Tradition and Revolution in Vietnam

Nguyen Khac Vien

Foreword by George McT. Kahin

Edited, with a preface by David Marr and Jayne Werner

Translation by Linda Yarr, Jayne Werner and Tran Tuong Nhu

Production by Keith Ervin

Additional assistance: Christine Keller, Ellen Trablicy, Christopher Jenkins, Tran Khanh Tuyet, Archetype Typesetting Collective, Katipunan ng mga Demokratikong Pilipino.

The Indochina Resource Center is an independent research group and information clearinghouse on contemporary Vietnam, Laos and Cambodia. Data and analysis often otherwise unavailable to the public are disseminated via newsletters, articles, books, audio-visual materials, seminars, briefings, and servicing of specific requests. Co-directors are David Marr and Fred Branfman.

Cover: The background is from a traditional popular print of Trieu Thi Trinh, who led a revolt against the Chinese colonial rulers in 248 A.D. In the foreground, a National Liberation Front militiawoman moves out on patrol somewhere in South Vietnam. (Design by Public Interest Communications.)

Contents

Foreword

Although by now a considerable number of Europeans and Americans interested in Vietnam have discovered the usefulness of Dr. Nguyen Khac Vien's *Vietnam Courier* and his widely ranging series, *Vietnamese Studies*, few are likely to have become familiar with his own writings, and the high standard they set. The present compilation brings together some of his best essays. Particularly valuable, I believe, for those interested in Vietnamese nationalism and the social and political dynamics underlying the formation and progress of the Democratic Republic of Vietnam will be the two major essays here included: "Confucianism and Marxism in Vietnam," and "Water, Rice and Men," first published in 1962, and 1963 respectively.

In the first of these essays, Dr. Vien provides illuminating insights into the way some of the tenets of an unofficial, non-establishment level of Confucianism (not to be confused with the official level that preoccupied Paul Mus) helped develop the sort of socio-psychological attitudes at the village level of Vietnamese society that inclined its members to be the more receptive to an ordering of society along socialist lines. He sees Confucianism as having left its mark on some aspects of Marxist thought in both China and Vietnam; and observes that "among the great family of Communist parties, the Vietnamese and Chinese have particularly exhibited more of a moralistic tone than Communist parties elsewhere, where the bourgeoisie has exercised ideological leadership over a long period of time." Whatever the current attitude towards Confucianism in other countries, Vietnamese Marxists appear to consider it "as part of their national heritage, to be assimilated by the new society."

In "Water, Rice and Men," Dr. Vien gives us a lucidly written account of the modern social history of a province in the delta of the Red River that constitutes something of a microhistory of the Vietnamese revolution. In a very literal sense he brings a phase of modern Vietnamese history "down to earth," to the village level and the point of view of its peasants. He depicts clearly, and in very human terms, the formidable economic and social problems encountered by the Vietnamese Communists, and their mistakes as well as their successes in attempting to solve them. Perhaps of particular interest to social scientists is his description of the role of local party cadres and organizations in developing and sustaining social mobilization for agricultural production and the building of irrigation facilities.

But, of course, it has not been the pattern of social organization as such that has accounted for the impressive achievements of the people of northern Vietnam. As I believe comes across in these essays, without the spirit and personal qualities of individual Vietnamese their society could not have attained its strength and resilience. Indeed, in reading through these pages I could not help but recall some of the most vivid of the impressions that registered in my mind during visits to the North in 1971 and 1972; that here was a social solidarity so strong as to be almost palpable; and a people whose conditioning by long struggle in the face of enormous adversity had left them with a quiet, dignified courage; a poised, steadfast confidence; and — despite the enormity of immediate problems — the capacity to see the present in perspective and to look ahead with an abiding optimism towards the ultimate accomplishment of long-term goals. Those who read this collection of Dr. Vien's essays are likely to come away with some appreciation of these qualities.

This slim volume constitutes a welcome and refreshing contribution towards offsetting the heavy dependency of Americans on Western perceptions of Vietnam. Those interested in a deeper understanding of that country, and especially of the way in which Vietnamese view their own recent history, will undoubtedly share my own sense of gratitude to Dr. David Marr and Jayne Werner for editing this collection of Dr. Vien's writings and to Linda Yarr, Jayne Werner and Tran Tuong Nhu for their excellent translations.

George McT. Kahin
May 1974

Preface

By David Marr and Jayne Werner

Nguyen Khac Vien is uniquely qualified to interpret Vietnam to a Western audience. Indeed, Europeans have been familiar with his writings for almost two decades now. They, like we, are constantly struck by his ability to combine acute observation, autobiographical reflection and penetrating analysis. Because he knows the West first-hand, almost as well as he knows his own country, Dr. Vien also has a seemingly unlimited reservoir of comparative examples and metaphors to make the Vietnamese experience more accessible, more tangible to foreigners.

Yet today there may not be one hundred Americans who recognize the name of Nguyen Khac Vien. This volume of translations is designed to remedy that defect. More than that, however, we believe that the writings contained in this slim book have the potential of raising discussion on Vietnam in the United States to a new level. Specialists may or may not agree with what Dr. Vien has to say, but henceforth they will find him almost impossible to ignore. The public ar large, long conditioned to American journalistic and behavioristic treatments of Vietnam, now has the opportunity to begin fathoming who the Vietnamese "enemy" really has been, why a whole series of U.S. presidents have sought to destroy the Vietnamese revolution, and, above all, why every such attempt has ended in dismal failure.

*   *   *   *   *

Born in 1913 the son of a mandarin official, Nguyen Khac Vien spent much of his childhood in a quiet village in north-central Vietnam, deeply appreciative of rural agrarian values, yet by his own admission largely oblivious to the social and political tensions and grievances around him. He attended French-language schools and received his baccalaureate at age 19. Then, following his father's advice not to make the same mistakes as himself, Nguyen Khac Vien decided to avoid the French colonial bureaucracy and to study for a career in medicine. (At that time the University of Hanoi offered degrees only in law — leading to the mandarinate — and in medicine.) Training in colonial schools,

David Marr is author of Vietnamese Anticolonialism *and is co-director of the Indochina Resource Center. Jayne Werner is writing a Ph.D. dissertation on Vietnam for Cornell University and recently returned from a visit to the Democratic Republic of Vietnam, where she had the opportunity to talk with Nguyen Khac Vien.*

he later commented wryly, failed to erase a very traditional notion "engrained deeply in myself and each of my peers, which was how we could repay the debt we owed our country and our society. In the past, becoming a mandarin, assuming a political function, was the supreme means to do so. The colonial regime blocked this path. Becoming a doctor would enable me to make an honorable, living while 'doing good.' I dreamed of treating my compatriots free of charge, since most of them were living in the most squalid misery."[1]

However, Nguyen Khac Vien soon discovered that patients who came to the hospitals to be treated often returned, suffering the same malady as before. Hunger, lack of sanitation, lack of education, and the general wretchedness of Vietnamese colonial society made a doctor's "good deeds" almost meaningless. Perhaps partly for this reason, he left for France to pursue advanced studies, and for a while the stimulation of rigorous scientific investigation, clinical analysis and diagnosis kept him occupied. Yet his mind invariably returned to the millions of his fellow-countrymen suffering from malaria, beriberi, tuberculosis and other diseases. He might learn how to cure each of these, indeed unravel all the secrets of medical science, "but as long as the colonial regime existed, these capabilities would act as cautery upon a wooden leg." He decided that the best medicine for Vietnam was national independence and he would worry about becoming a good doctor later.

Unfortunately, Dr. Vien was struck with a very serious case of tuberculosis himself. He was operated on six times; one lung had to be removed. He spent ten years in French sanitariums, at the end of which time medical experts gave him 36 months to live. Refusing to accept their verdict as final, yet knowing that there was nothing more "Western" medicine could do, Dr. Vien embarked on a rigorous study,

---

[1]Nguyen Khac Vien, "Quelques souvenirs personnels," *Bulletin d'information et de documentation,* Association d'Amitié Franco-Vietnamienne, June 1973, p. 8.

exercise and dieting program derived from new investigations and testing of texts on "Eastern," or Chinese and Vietnamese, medicine. The key to his system, he wrote later, was to relate the mind, the muscles and the body organs to each other, to train oneself in such a way that these three elements were always mutually sustaining and reinforcing.[2] Today, some 16 years after he was expected to die, Dr. Vien carries on.

During the 1950s, still in France and still in precarious health, Dr. Vien was a prominent leader of the Movement of Vietnamese Patriots—forerunner of a much larger organization which today is called the Union of Vietnamese in France.[3] Since the Movement supported the Vietnamese independence movement and was resolutely anticolonial, Dr. Vien and his fellow members faced perpetual harassment by the French police. When they tried to establish a library of books and study documents on Vietnam and the Vietnamese revolution, they were forced to shift locations and addresses constantly, which made the endeavor nearly impossible. Harassment continued even after the signing of the 1954 Geneva Accords because France retained significant interests in South Vietnam and because progressive Vietnamese were known to have formed contacts with the Algerian FLN. Nevertheless, Dr. Vien traveled assiduously for speaking engagements and wrote often in such publications as *La Pensée, La Nouvelle Démocratie* and *La Nouvelle Critique*. It is a little-known fact, but without the intimate friendship of

[2] Dr. Vien has written a lucid pamphlet on the subject for his countrymen, entitled *Ren Luyen Co The, Ren Luyen Con Nguoi* (Forging the Body, Forging the Person), Paris, December 1973.

[3] The Union of Vietnamese in France presently has at least 3,000 full-fledged members and enjoys support from another 5,000 overseas Vietnamese. It publishes a well-prepared, informative newspaper titled *Doan Ket* (Unity), and maintains working contacts with similar but smaller Vietnamese groups in other Western European and North American countries.

Vietnamese laborers—many of them residing in France from the time of the First World War—Dr. Vien could never have accomplished what he did.

In 1961, a quarter century after his departure, Dr. Vien returned to the northern part of Vietnam—the Democratic Republic of Vietnam (DRV). Still in frail health, he nonetheless undertook tasks of considerable importance. He became editor of the *Etudes Vietnamiennes* research series and of the periodical *Courrier du Vietnam*. The former, available in English as *Vietnamese Studies*, has now reached a total of 37 paperbound issues, ranging from U.S. "special warfare" techniques to the Vietnamese literary classic, *The Tale of Kieu*. The latter journal, printed as *Vietnam Courier* in English, now comes out every month and is a major source of information and interpretation. Recently, Dr. Vien became responsible for all DRV foreign-language publications.

With such preoccupations, not to mention traveling throughout the DRV and contributing to European journals, such as *Le Monde Diplomatique,* Dr. Vien has obviously been unable to return to full-time medical practice. However, medicine in the DRV has not stood still in his absence, as he is the first to point out with pride:

> Today, when a case of malaria or beriberi is discovered, professors and students gather to examine it as if it were a rare disease. Today's students rarely see a syphilitic canker or a phagedenic ulcer except in books. They have difficulty understanding my surprise. As I look around nowadays I find that, materially, life has not changed much. Thirty years of war have not let us turn over a completely new leaf. Nevertheless, a new science of pathology is available to young doctors today. They no longer treat the same diseases. The humanitarian dreams of young doctors are no longer blocked by the desperate vision of the powerlessness of medicine.[4]

*   *   *   *   *

[4] Nguyen Khac Vien, "Quelques souvenirs personnels," p. 9.

In 1970, the French publishing house, *Editions Sociales*, brought together a number of Nguyen Khac Vien's articles and essays and published them under the title *Expériences Vietnamiennes*. Four of the essays translated here are from that book. *Expériences Vietnamiennes* was received with great enthusiasm in Europe, not only because readers knew of the author's reputation, but because really for the first time someone was giving them an insight into the Vietnamese *Weltanschauung*, or world view. *Expériences Vietnamiennes* treats many of the same cultural and social issues as the much-hailed *Sociologie d'une Guerre* by Paul Mus, but conclusions and style differ markedly. Nguyen Khac Vien, being Vietnamese and having been personally involved in the struggle for national independence, achieves both an intimate perception of traditional values and an understanding of revolutionary change that Paul Mus lacked. Moreover, he positions the Vietnamese struggle within a global political context, something Mus chose not to do.

In this first English-language edition of Nguyen Khac Vien's work, we begin with a relatively recent essay, retitled "Some Reflections on Ending the War." Written shortly after the January 27, 1973 signing of the Paris Agreement, it represents a very personal attempt to convey what the agreement meant and how he felt about the withdrawal of American troops, the first time that Vietnamese soil was unsullied by the boots of alien soldiers in more than a century. In light of events of the past year, particularly continuing violations of the agreement by Saigon and the United States, some readers will perhaps feel that Dr. Vien was excessively optimistic. Nevertheless, we suspect he sticks firmly to his basic prognosis.

The next selection, "The Judo Lesson," is Dr. Vien's brief, almost poetic explanation of how a small, ill-equipped people can hope to defeat a huge, technologically sophisticated adversary, providing the correct principles are applied. It also serves to introduce a dominant theme in his writings: the manner in which Vietnam has grown by tapping both traditional cultural roots and modern revolutionary doctrine. This theme is given historical and intellectual solidity in Dr. Vien's subsequent analysis of "Confucianism and Marxism in Vietnam." While not necessarily the last word on the subject, this essay does demonstrate how the Vietnamese have tended to remold and refine foreign concepts according to their own lights, their own specific requirements. Dr. Vien tries to avoid abstraction, bringing both traditional and Marxist eras to life with sharp examples and anecdotes.

It is interesting to contrast Dr. Vien's personal contemplations on the positive moral legacy of certain Confucian teachings with the severe, seemingly total rejection of Confucius in the People's Republic of China. Two ideas may be ventured on this subject for the reader to think about while reading this essay. First of all, the apparent contrast between Vietnamese and Chinese attitudes toward Confucius probably reflects the fact that Vietnam never accepted the old gentleman and his disciples quite as unequivocally as did China, the land of his birth. Nor did the local landed gentry in Vietnam ever succeed in controlling provincial education and institutionalizing power to the degree often found in China.

Secondly, however, it will not come as a surprise to us if the question of "feudal attitudes" — not only Confucian but others as well — is reasserted strongly at some future date in Vietnam, perhaps when the imperialist threat abates in intensity. For example, are there lingering attitudes toward women in Vietnamese society posing obstacles to future development and progress? Are there tendencies toward bureaucracy and status-seeking that can be ascribed at least in part to traditional ruler-mandarin-subject reflexes? Even the Vietnamese language continues to militate against equality, due to certain hierarchical distinctions built into its very structure.

On the other hand, Vietnam may well have attacked and surmounted its most critical feudal problems in the impassioned debates of the 1930s (after the founding of the Indochinese Communist Party), the 1945 August Revolution, and the land reform of the late 1950s. Nguyen Khac Vien provides evidence for this in his carefully-researched "Water, Rice and Men." Here Dr. Vien is able to bring his enviable talents as a scientific observer to bear on one Red River delta province, Hung Yen, reconstructing the horror and degradation of colonial conditions, documenting improvements occurring as a result of independence, the land reform and the formation of agricultural cooperatives, and explaining in detail what remains to be done. Although written in late 1963, more than ten years ago, "Water, Rice and Men" is still the most perceptive and informative "provincial history" to come out of Vietnam, North or South.[5] In terms of analysis, this essay is to Vietnam in many ways what *Fanshen* is to China. Many of the aspirations and concrete plans mentioned by Dr. Vien have had to be repeatedly deferred, due to the intervening Vietnamese defense against massive American intervention and bombing, and are only now being implemented.

Lest readers be somehow misled into thinking that Vietnam is totally unique, Dr. Vien has written a provocative essay on "The Vietnamese Experience and the Third World."[6] Once again we see the tremendous technological gap which still exists in Vietnam and other third world countries, yet also the quiet confidence displayed by the working class and peasants—not the bourgeoisie—in leading the revolution to overcome poverty and backwardness. There is no flamboyant rhetoric here, simply a critical appraisal of the important choices that all underdeveloped countries have to make.

[5] A partial update of Dr. Vien's findings on Hung Yen (now part of Hai Hung province) can be found in Gerard Chaliand, *The Peasants of North Vietnam* (Baltimore: Penguin Books, 1969).

[6] Originally Dr. Vien used the term *"les pays sous-développés"* (underdeveloped countries). As will be seen in his interview with *Jeune Afrique*, however, he accepts *"le tiers monde,"* or third world, as the more current expression.

Nguyen Khac Vien's ability to communicate with third world peoples, not just Europeans, is further demonstrated in "The American War: An Interview with *Jeune Afrique (Young Africa).*" As one of the *Jeune Afrique* editors remarked in an introductory comment, Dr. Vien "struck us above all by the rigor and clarity of his presentation, often enhanced by personal vignettes, and by the quiet sureness with which he explained the unshakeable will of a people to overcome the most atrocious suffering." In this interview, held in Paris just after the 1973 peace agreement was signed, Dr. Vien outlines the various stages of U.S. escalation in Vietnam and gives his own perspective on American imperialism. Even some blunt questions about the "socialist camp," in particular the Soviet Union, are handled by Dr. Vien with aplomb if not complete resolution.

"The Old Banyan Tree," another of Dr. Vien's classic essays, rich in metaphor and simple in style, is included by way of summary and conclusion to this English-language edition. The author provides a touching statement of what it was like to be the son of a mandarin growing up well-fed and happy, oblivious to the dark, desperate side of peasant existence. He admits that he really did not know the peasants of his country until they had taken power in their own right, in the process of which his family, along with many others, was stripped of its special privileges and property. The myth that peasants are indolent and apolitical is brought to rest here.

*   *   *   *   *

Through these writings Nguyen Khac Vien emerges as an extremely sensitive social commentator—one might almost say social philosopher, except that he would blush at the characterization. Yet, like the best of philosophers, Dr. Vien has an overpowering urge to consume every possible sensory impression, to define, to organize thoughts, to analyze and to draw conclusions of real value to his own society and also, hopefully, of universal significance as well. Doing this for Vietnam does not mean that he has lost touch with the rest of the world. On the contrary, Dr. Vien keeps a close monitor on world events and current intellectual controversies—no small achievement given the state of technology in the DRV, his tight budget, bombs having fallen on his library, and the government priorities given to total mobilization, defense and, more recently, rehabilitation and reconstruction. During the past year he has been investigating the trauma in South Vietnamese society caused by the presence of two and a half million American troops who came and went from 1965 to 1973. He has already published several brief articles on this subject in *Vietnam Courier*, pointing out that continuing U.S. involvement and support of the Thieu regime serves only to perpetuate the neo-colonial disease.

Finally, perhaps we should say what Nguyen Khac Vien is not. Having been out of Vietnam during the critical period of armed resistance to the French (1945-54), it should be apparent that he is not equipped to write on revolutionary doctrine or strategies of guerrilla warfare with the experience of a Truong Chinh or a Vo Nguyen Giap. Nor would he ever presume to define and delineate *Lao Dong* (Workers') Party and DRV government policies with the authority of a Le Duan or a Pham Van Dong. And Dr. Vien cannot be compared in cultural terms with, for example, To Huu, Vietnam's greatest living poet and also, not incidentally, a respected member of the Party Secretariat.

For all these reasons, and also because no single human being can ever encompass all that has happened in recent decades, we present this collection of essays not as any definitive picture of Vietnam (nor even as full measure of Dr. Vien's capacities), but rather as the first in what we expect will be a series of translations of Vietnamese perceptions of their own land and people. We can immediately think of five or six contemporary Vietnamese writers who deserve equal attention. Dr. Vien could easily mention ten or twenty more.

Unfortunately, it is not that simple. Aside from the energy involved in translating and publishing such works, there is the fact that most of these authors seldom if ever write with foreign readers in mind. Hence, to appreciate them requires a much higher level of cross-cultural knowledge than has existed in the United States up to now.

Thus, it is no accident that we have selected Nguyen Khac Vien first. Although his presentation is hardly the sum total of the Vietnamese experience, traditional or revolutionary, it is an important, indeed crucial step forward, toward whatever quotient of understanding one people may hope or desire to have of another. Dr. Vien sets a high standard of excellence. We know he will be working with others to continue the achievements reflected in this book.

Some Reflections
on Ending The War

Children are romping in the street and in a brightly-lit restaurant people are busily talking to each other. The ear, usually alerted to the roar of jets overhead or to the wail of alarm sirens, needs some time to get used to the sounds of peace. Peace has arrived, but you rub your eyes to wonder if indeed it is here.

Could it be true that our people, our country, Vietnam, this little place on the world map, has been able to drive back the superpowerful America? More than 200 billion dollars, or the equivalent of 50 years of hard work by the entire Vietnamese people, both North and South, have fallen on our land, our heads, our hearts, in the form of bombs, shells and napalm, instruments of corruption and terror—and yet we have survived, we have held out, we have won. Can this be true?

I cannot help looking at and examining the gait and face of each of my fellow-countrymen that I pass: my neighbor, a frail young woman who used to ride her bike every Sunday to visit her children evacuated from Hanoi; the soldier sauntering by on leave, looking quite relaxed, probably weighing no more than 110 pounds; the brown-clad peasant, barefooted, coming to town for a bit of shopping; my friend T.H.,[1] the poet, pondering his verses as he takes a walk along the street. I ask myself what made it possible for us to resist and win. It was nothing belligerent, nor did it reveal much of a warrior's spirit. It was simply a great calmness of mind and a good-natured twinkle in the eyes at all times, even under a deluge of bombs.

Twenty-three years have passed, years that have marked in a very deep way our national history and perhaps the history of the entire world in the twentieth century. Indeed, 23 years have rolled by since the day two American cruisers docked in Saigon harbor to show the French that the U.S.A. was on their side—23 years since our people started a direct confrontation with American power. On that day, our people found the way to force American warships to leave the port by demonstrating by the hundreds of thousands in the streets of Saigon.

Since then, each Vietnamese has come to know the names of the American presidents one after the other— Truman, Eisenhower, Kennedy, Johnson, Nixon—whose five reigns were five ways of making war on our people. Old-style

---

[1] Almost surely a reference to To Huu, probably the greatest Vietnamese poet of the twentieth century.—*Ed.*

This essay is adapted from "Light and Shadow, Vietnam Courier, *February 1973.*

colonial war, with French soldiers and American weapons and money; unilateral war, with massacres, tortures and mop-up raids under Ngo Dinh Diem, while our people, in observance of the 1954 Geneva Accords, had put aside their weapons; special war, with U.S. advisers and strategic hamlets; then fully Americanized war; and finally Vietnamized war, with its million puppet troops and the unbridled fury of American air and naval power.

That Hitler's Germany could savagely attack the Soviet Union might be explained. But why should Washington vent its fury on this little country, Vietnam? In what way did our people threaten the vital interests of the United States? Why did five successive American presidents seek to crush us by any means possible? There can be only one answer to all these questions. American imperialism nurses vast designs, and its way to world hegemony passes through the conquest and subjugation of the third world. It so happened that Vietnam was giving a bad example by stubbornly refusing to allow itself to be dominated and assimilated, by being determined to preserve its integrity and independence. This black sheep, this alien element, this unfortunate pebble on the road, had to be eliminated at all costs, at any cost. The best American brains—engineers, scientists, sociologists, economists, ethnologists, churchmen—were mobilized to this end. The Vietnamese people went through many trials: B-52s, steel-pellet bombs, laser-guided bombs, election farces, tiger cages, operations Phoenix and Swan. Just think: two hundred billion dollars! And the most extraordinary thing of all is that it failed!

I shall always remember the look of surprise on the faces of some of my foreign interviewers when I told them that the Americans were going from one defeat to another in Vietnam. How's that? The Vietnamese were the ones who were being bombed, whose towns were destroyed and whose countrymen decimated. So how was it that the Americans were being defeated? My interviewers were even more amazed when I told them that the Vietnamese people were on the offensive and the Americans were being driven to the defensive. How could they be on the defensive when they were sending thousands of aircraft to bomb their adversary? And yet, what verdict other than that of defeat could be handed down on the wrestler who has used every means at his disposal against his opponent, but eventually has to give up, leaving the other man standing on his feet? All-powerful America used all the mechanical, aeronautical, chemical, electronic and cybernetic resources at its command. It was not far from achieving its ideal of a fully-automated war. On October 16, 1969, addressing the American Congress, General Westmoreland said jubilantly:

> Enemy forces will be located, tracked and targeted almost instantaneously through the use of data links, computer-assisted intelligence evaluation, and automated fire control . . . . I see battlefields or combat areas that are under 24-hour real or near real time surveillance of all types. I see battlefields on which we can destroy almost anything we locate through instant communications and the almost instantaneous application of highly lethal firepower.

That confidence, not to say intoxication, of General Westmoreland, was the same for Rostow, Taylor, Robert Thompson and Samuel Huntington, in short all those whose business it was to devise the politico-military tactics and strategies for Washington. They used the most terrifying armaments and the most refined political, police, financial, ideological methods—who could win against them? I can imagine what it must have been like for these men, who had expected the NLF and PRG to be knocked out in the first round, to wake up to the harsh reality that the NLF and the PRG of South Vietnam were more vigorous and solid than ever. In fact, the NLF and the PRG spoke to these representatives of the great America on an equal footing and put forth reasonable yet firm demands. And there they were, relaxed and confident, allies of the North Vietnam that these men had expected to bomb back to the Stone Age after only a few raids.

What could they do, now that technology had proven ineffective, now that carefully-elaborated strategies and policies had gone bankrupt? Should the grand design of colonizing two-thirds of the world be given up? For many years, the great America had had no other war to wage but the one in Vietnam, and yet it failed to win that one. While it was bogged down in the Indochina quagmire, its sworn enemies and its allies, too, who were nevertheless dangerous rivals, were making giant strides on both the economic and military planes.

Not only did Washington fail to win, but it was left with a torn-up society, a youth gnawed by doubt, an army corrupted by drug abuse and haunted by crimes committed in Vietnam, cities more polluted than ever, runaway crime and a threatened dollar. How could all these problems be solved? Didn't their existence show that America was truly on the defensive?

In my mind's eye, I still see the America of the fifties, an object of fear and envy for the whole world. The myth that America was a model of power, organization and a new way of life was sustained by A- and H-bomb explosions, by daily news reports appearing on movie and television screens all over the world featuring colossal rockets and gigantic aircraft carriers. It was fed by an apparently unassailable dollar, by innumerable grants and loans, and by a multitude of charitable, academic and religious missions. But where do these stand after years of war in Vietnam?

Perhaps the greatest loss for American imperialism can be found in its loss of confidence in itself, the irremediable loss of the illusion of its omnipotence, and the total change in the way the world feels about American invincibility. But perhaps a new starting point for America can also be found there: for scientists, workers, students, men and women of peace and progress, who will mark out and be the true America, a fresh starting point from which to think and rebuild a future no longer in terms of domination, but of justice and human solidarity. I am quite aware that Mr. Nixon has not suddenly become a gentle dove, and that the military-industrial complex still firmly holds the reins of power. But from among those acute and numerous contradictions now renting American society, the chances are equal, I think, for either an exacerbated fascism or for high hopes to spring forth. New ideas have been germinated in the heads and hearts of millions of Americans, and they may develop more rapidly than anyone may imagine.

We too have lost a great deal, but we have made enormous gains. How many are our dead, our wounded, our invalids? How long will the physical, moral and psychological consequences of this war last? How long will it take to rebuild our cities and villages? How will we make up for the technological lag which has accumulated over all these years because of the war? We shall, of course, have to face attempts to corrupt and subvert us and the war threats of American imperialism, which will surely not slacken in pressure. My head swims when I think of all those problems of the distant and near future! Especially engraved in my mind is the memory of that child in Haiphong who lost both his hands in an air raid: what will he do with the rest of his life? I also think of a friend of mine, a native of the South regrouped to the North after 1954, whose hair turned white when he learned that his son, whom he had left behind at the age of three, and with whom he thought he would be reunited in 1956, had recently become a torturer in the service of the Americans. I think of those white headbands for mourning in our villages and in our cities,[2] and of our forests which will take 20 years to recover.

But whenever I close my eyes and try to picture the future, I always see light, and under my feet I feel the firm ground on which we will build. I see the past 28 years unfold again as if they were in a film: 1945, the August Revolution;

---

[2] The Vietnamese wear white in mourning.—*Ed.*

1954, Dien Bien Phu; 1973, the victory over American aggression. Our people have truly put on the giant's seven-league boots. I remember the somber period of 1954-59 when the Saigon regime was carrying out a wholesale massacre of our southern militants and countrymen, when the national movement was waning and the South appeared lost. It is we who are at the end of the tunnel. We will always have our mountains and rivers and especially our men and women who have matured in the process. We shall rebuild our country ten times more beautiful . This is not just a promise: for me it is a reality.

My thoughts irresistibly turn to those years in the thirteenth century when our forefathers drove out the Mongolian armies, which were the most powerful of the time. We have shown ourselves to be worthy of our ancestors. We have kept that great national tradition intact; and what is more, we have socialism, that new type of yeast which has increased our centuries-old national consciousness tenfold.

I look at my young daughter who is reading a difficult text in the light of a kerosene lamp, electric power not yet having been fully restored. I know that her generation will see a blossoming greater than our own. We shall not have gone through these sufferings and hardships in vain.

The Judo Lesson

The puny little man was wracking his brain trying to figure out a way to overcome his opponent's mass of muscle and brawn. None of the weaker man's punches seemed to have the slightest effect, whereas the stronger boxer needed only to flex a finger to stun his adversary and knock him out. It was really a quandary.

The judo teacher arrived. "Your opponent," he explained, "is movement. It is in that same movement, not in your own strength, that you must find the force to defeat your opponent. Grab his moves at the end of their thrust, prolong them, and you will lure your adversary into a fall which he himself has precipitated.

"Of course," the teacher continued, "you will have to give it all your strength. Until now you have not really discovered where your true strength lies. You try to punch, you pull your adversary by the arm to make him fall down. That's wrong! If you want to topple him, whack him on the side; don't pull him by the arms. If you really want to give it to him, do it with your foot, not your fists.

"The body has sensitive areas and vitally important reflex points. You must master the techniques of delivering the fatal blow to the proper spot if you want to finish off a dangerous adversary and engage in serious combat. You must acquire a thorough knowledge of the working of the human body if you want to become a judo master."

*   *   *   *   *

For many long years I witnessed the highly emotional, historically important judo match taking place in my country, almost without penetrating the principles involved.

My first memories go back to 1930.

I was a schoolboy in Vinh. People were dying by the thousands from famine. One day, a mob of six or seven thousand peasants in rags, brandishing sticks, headed toward town. It seemed as if all the villages surrounding Vinh had been depopulated of their women, children and old people, like ant hills after a storm. The mob advanced relentlessly to town where the French functionaries and the mandarins rushed to barricade themselves in their offices.

All of a sudden a plane flew over these thousands of people, circling several times over the heads of the famished crowd and then—tac, tac, tac!—spat out its deadly fire. What indescribable panic! A few hours later, silence returned to the

First published in 1961, this article has been translated from Expériences Vietnamiennes, *Nguyen Khac Vien (Paris: Editions Sociales, 1971).*

area where several hundred corpses lay.

During the next few years, each time I heard my friends at the University of Hanoi discussing the regaining of our country's independence, I would look at these frail and elegant young men from good families and ask myself: what could they have done if they had been confronted by that airplane? I did not realize then that planes would become less and less efficient as the masses began to stir.

Then I set sail for Marseilles. I was fascinated with the port from the start. Cranes were poised for several miles along the docks, boats rocking against each other, trucks and trains rumbling along the wharves. This profusion of machinery, steel and technical power overwhelmed me. I thought of our villages, where no one had even seen a screw. I thought of my father, who never stopped telling us that we might dream of independence but our country had to import even nails, which we were unable to make ourselves.

We were weak and poor. A single plane could disperse crowds. The technique of manufacturing nails escaped us completely. All of this obsessed me for years and years. I saw that neither of those two elder Asian statesmen, Gandhi or Sun Yat-sen, could teach me how to silence an armed plane with my bare hands, or how to make nails which would not break. I reread the history of my country, which showed me that our resistance to foreign domination had never ceased. But while men might die heroes and insurrections and uprisings might occur one after another, the colonial regime might never be toppled.

Our scholars, in the name of Confucius and the Emperor, led the peasants to battle against the French, fighting exactly as our ancestors had fought against the feudal Chinese armies. But these methods were sheer absurdity in the face of planes and the likes of Colonel Gallieni and General Lyautey. Attempts by our bourgeoisie and petty bourgeoisie in the towns, in plotting other uprisings, were even more ludicrous. The Yen Bay insurrection was wiped out in a single night.[1]

*   *   *   *   *

Ho Chi Minh and Lenin showed us the way.

Imperialism is the highest stage of capitalism. Lenin taught us that imperialism is a system vastly more powerful than any system of the past. Amateurs and ignorant people should not play at the struggle against it. Imperialism, because of its evolutionary process, is fraught with contradictions. . Revolutionaries must know how to prepare themselves so that they will be ready when these contradictions burst, to seize upon them, to break the weakest link of the system.

This notion of internal contradictions within imperialism is crucial. Without it, there would be no chance for the struggle to succeed. In Vietnam our scholars fought without the capacity to win. But with the founding in 1930 of the Indochinese Communist Party, which had barely 300 members, a new spirit was born among the militants in the national movement. Divested of everything, isolated in the midst of the still unconscious masses, these militants had the confidence of those who are sure of final victory. The Confucian scholar on the execution block repeated, "I die, but I have fulfilled my duty." The militant communist, facing a firing squad, said, "I die, but you will be defeated," and thought, "When the contradictions come to a head, we will be there and we will win."

Confucian scholar-gentry and the bourgeoisie saw the nation as a homogeneous bloc. Marx and Lenin taught us that, even here, there is movement and contradiction. Study the makeup of your country well and study how different social classes behave toward foreign domination. What are

[1] Insurrection against French troops in the garrison of Yen Bay in 1930, organized by the Vietnam Nationalist Party (*Vietnam Quoc Dan Dang*). —Ed.

their interests, their ambitions, their ideas about the future?
Find out first of all what social class a person represents,
whatever his statements or apparent beliefs, and you will
have the means to determine the correct posture to take
toward him.

Pay particular attention to workers and poor peasants.
When these people acquire national consciousness and class
consciousness, the match will be won. The critical strength of
the revolutionary movement lies in them.

Confucianism and Marxism in Vietnam

Albert Camus once said he thought that world peace could be achieved only if men of good will from all over the world would form a universal brotherhood like that of Confucian scholars and take their inspiration from Confucian doctrine. I asked him what basis he had for thinking that in today's world Confucianism could help to establish international peace. "According to the Confucian texts I've been able to read, they could," Camus answered.

"Confucianism," I said, "was an integral part of a particular society. Do you really think it could be taken out of its social and historical context and used again today?

Throwing his hands in the air, Camus replied, "What do

you expect? All I know of Confucianism comes from texts, and besides, I am not a historical materialist."

For Albert Camus, Confucianism was one doctrine among many he encountered by chance in reading. As with any great doctrine, one can always find the means to form grand opinions on man and the world. For the Vietnamese, however, Confucianism represents much more than a doctrine inscribed in venerable texts; it is a legacy of history, a fundamental legacy to be understood, fought against and overcome in the course of the historical change which the country is now undergoing.

The author of this essay belongs to those generations of Vietnamese who, even in grammar school, learned history from the little textbook by Ernest Lavisse, which mentioned "our ancestors, the Gauls." The Confucian texts were no longer taught in the schools we went to. Our fathers, uncles and elders, however, were either mandarins or scholars and were all imbued with Confucianism. Therefore, all the pressures of Confucian orthodoxy were brought to bear on our youth, and in the name of Confucius we were denied a number of things. We were also required to conform to innumerable tests of discipline. Above all, Confucianism was something that was lived. On the columns of houses, on engravings, on the doors of monuments, inscriptions reminded us at each step of the teachings of the Confucian tradition. Confucian expressions and quotations abounded in everyday language as well as in literature.

There were debates on the pros and cons of Confucianism. But people in my generation still got a first-hand knowledge of the classic Confucian man, the scholar. With his

First published in La Pensée, *No. 105, October, 1962, this article also appeared in* Tradition et Révolution au Vietnam, *Chesneaux, Boudarel and Hemery, eds. (Paris: Editions Anthropos, 1971); and in* Expériences Vietnamiennes, *Nguyen Khac Vien (Paris: Editions Sociales, 1971).*

black turban, ceremonial gestures and flowery manner of speech, the exact opposite of the peasant, worker or laborer, or the debonair modern young man, he elicited repulsion as well as respect. We were repulsed by the outmoded, fossilized side of his character, but we respected him for something undefinable, something those of us educated in the Western school felt we lacked, not understanding precisely why.

They never stopped haranguing us about our Confucian past. We were told we should nurture the positive aspects of our tradition and reject the negative ones. This drugstore remedy was not terribly useful. How were we supposed to tell which were positive aspects and which were negative? We were given almost no criteria to recognize either aspect or a practical method by which to make such a selection. Yet our struggle against the Confucian system, including its positive side, became a practical problem that could not be reduced to a simple matter of studying the texts.

Landowning Peasants and Mandarins

Confucianism was the official doctrine of the imperial examinations in traditional Vietnam. The first examination was held in 1075 and the last took place in 1919. For ten centuries Confucianism was the intellectual and ideological backbone of Vietnam. The Vietnamese monarchy recruited its high officials according to the results of these competitive examinations, which were open to all persons except theatrical people and, of course, women. These exams included essay questions on literature, ethics and politics, poetry composition, and the writing of administrative texts.

Regional examinations conferred degrees which, for want of better terms, we shall call baccalaureates and licentiates. Students holding the latter degree had the right to take the imperial examinations given in the capital city, under the high authority of the Emperor himself. These examinations led to the doctoral degree. Students who passed the regional and imperial examinations could be appointed to administrative positions, become mandarins, executors of the imperial will, and members of a regime which administered the entire kingdom.

There was no place to house the thousands of students who thronged the regional centers for the tests, so each one came with a tent and a slate and set himself up with all the others in a large field designated for this purpose. (Some of the old examination grounds are now being used as airfields.) At night, by the light of big torches, the roll call was taken and the candidates were admitted into the camp. The examinations began at dawn. From the tops of tall lookout towers, the mandarins who were monitoring the tests watched over the candidates, and militiamen patrolled to check any attempts at cheating.

Very few of the many candidates passed the tests, scarcely a hundred out of several thousand. In the whole period from 1075 to 1919, only slightly more than 2,000 doctoral degrees were granted. Those who earned their degrees ceremoniously received a hat and a large tunic as gifts from the Emperor. Returning to their native villages, they were welcomed with music and flags by the local authorities and the entire population. If it so pleased the degree-holder, he could rightfully lead the procession through anyone's field or garden, and cut down any hedge that might be in his way.

"Grinding" to become a mandarin had been for centuries the highest dream a boy could have, while the very best a girl from a good family could hope for was to marry a scholar on the chance that he would one day accede to the mandarinate. (This long tradition explains why, to this day, Vietnamese students have never been afraid to take the entrance examinations to the French *Grandes Ecoles*.) All the young people were obsessed with the dream of passing the mandarinate exminations, the resultant prestige being far greater than admission to the *Polytéchnique* or *Normale supérieure* schools in France.

Passing the exams was much more than a scholarly success; the degree-holder left the ranks of the people to enter the mandarin "caste." Before he took the examination he lived like anyone else, but as a mandarin he went to live in the administrative buildings of the sub-prefectures, provinces and ministries. Today's civil servant sits behind his desk all day and then returns to his home. A feudal lord lived in his castle surrounded by ramparts and moats, completely separated from the people. The life of a mandarin was halfway between those of a feudal lord and of a modern civil servant: the mandarin's residence was both an administrative building and a family home. There were no ramparts, but there was a solid fence with militiamen on guard duty night and day. There was a long entourage of pages, valets and soldiers to tend to the wants of the feudal lord, but only a small number of state-paid guards served the mandarin. When the mandarin went out, he was followed by two or three guards carrying banners and a parasol. People cleared a path for him and greeted him respectfully. When an ordinary person went to see a mandarin, he didn't simply enter an office where an unimposing representative of the state stood behind a counter. On the contrary, he was confronted by a whole panoply of banners, insignia, coats of arms, and inscriptions in golden letters. An entire etiquette of gestures and compulsory verbal courtesies was used, and a person was obliged to bow his head. The ordinary person was in the presence of a representative of His Imperial Majesty.

*   *   *   *   *

The Ly dynasty, which had instituted the mandarin examinations in the eleventh century, was the first royal dynasty able to unite all the territory of Vietnam under its authority. Vietnam had achieved independence in the tenth century by liberating itself from Chinese feudal domination. Vietnam then needed a centralized monarchical state and a mandarin bureaucracy to administer the country for three reasons—to build an extensive network of dikes, to preserve national independence, and to guard against peasant revolts.

The Red River delta, cradle of Vietnamese civilization, was periodically threatened by great floods. In order to survive, the Vietnamese had to build thousands of miles of dikes along the river and all its tributaries. But before this could be accomplished, the rivalry of local feudal powers had to be ended. Only when peace was achieved could a centralized administration be established to supervise the construction and maintenance of the dike network.

Furthermore, Vietnam was threatened by periodic attempts of Chinese feudal dynasties to reconquer the country, and the small, scattered fiefdoms would have been quickly absorbed by the Chinese. In the twelfth century the people struggled against the Chinese Sung dynasty; in the thirteenth century they pushed back the Mongol invasion, but only after mobilizing the entire country. In the beginning of the fifteenth century, the Chinese tried once again to reconquer Vietnam, and the resulting war of liberation lasted for ten years. And, late in the eighteenth century, the Ch'ing occupied the country with a large army. Under the leadership of the Tay Son, however, the Vietnamese people quickly chased away the invader.

The great water network, as well as the struggle for national independence, necessitated frequent mobilizations of the entire peasantry. Hundreds of thousands of people would assemble to work on the dikes. Because the Vietnamese monarchy could line up only a small number of regular troops to fight the huge Chinese feudal armies, the entire people had to be mobilized to defend the nation. These peasants, having conquered nature as well as invaders, would not be satisfied to return home and resume life under the conditions of slavery that had been imposed on them. The peasants' struggle for their rights weaves in and out of Vietnamese history like a piece of red thread. Unless we can grasp this concept of peasant struggle we cannot understand Vietnamese history.

Even after Vietnam had attained its independence in the tenth century, great feudal families still ruled, dividing the country among themselves, forcing serfs to cultivate the land on their fiefs and maintaining a large number of domestic slaves and private troops. From the eleventh to the fourteenth century, during which time the Ly and Tran kings unified the country, these feudal families, as well as members of the royal family and high dignitaries of the court, all continued to appropriate vast domains that sometimes comprised entire districts. They ruled thousands of serfs and often had private troops at their disposal. High state functions were reserved to princes of royal blood or to members of the great feudal families. Until the thirteenth century, Buddhism was the dominant religion; bonzes were counselors to the king, and Buddhist monasteries owned large domains cultivated by serfs.

Nonetheless, peasants had been fighting for their freedom and the right to own land privately for a long time. Some peasants did own their own land and cultivated it themselves in addition to the land appropriated by the monarchy or incorporated into the great feudal or monastic domains. While the peasantry as a whole continued to fight for the abolition of fiefdoms and for the expropriation of Buddhist monasteries, the peasant landowners assumed a more and more active historical role. The monarchy also had a vested interest in eliminating large feudal families. Then, toward the end of the thirteenth century, the victory over the Mongol invaders contributed to the demise of vast feudal and monastic domains. The entire peasantry, mobilized against a powerful enemy for years, gained freedom once the war was over, and the principle of private ownership of land became universal. Thus, after several centuries of struggle, the class of peasant landowners finally triumphed over the class of feudal lords. After the expropriation of monastic lands Buddhism was no longer the dominant religion. Confucianism took over.

In the beginning of the fifteenth century, Ming troops from China occupied the country, and a peasant landowner, Le Loi, organized a great national insurrection to liberate the country. His adviser, Nguyen Trai, was not a Buddhist bonze but a Confucian scholar, a politician, a writer, and a military strategist. During the Le dynasty Buddhism underwent its final decline, to be replaced by Confucianism. The monarchy had left high state functions to members of the royal family and the great feudal families, but now the administrative ranks were being filled by mandarins trained in the Confucian school and recruited on the basis of competitive examinations. At the same time that the peasants were fighting to abolish serfdom and attain private ownership of land, Confucian mandarins and scholars were gradually eliminating the feudal lords from the state apparatus and Buddhism from the ideological arena.

Several centuries of peasant struggle thus resulted in the creation of an agrarian society in which the class of peasant landowners predominated. This society was administered by a hereditary monarchy which still recruited its officials—the mandarins—by means of competitive examinations. In principle the rights to own land and to accede to the mandarinate were shared by all. But, in reality, only a minority was able to acquire land. Most peasants, although legally free, were forced to till other people's land. The class of peasant landowners, the mandarin bureaucracy, and the absolute, hereditary monarchy adopted Confucianism as their ideology.

Communal Life and Village Scholars

With fiefdoms eliminated, the king reigned and the mandarins administered, but the Vietnamese state had far to go before it would be a nation in the modern sense of the word. The techniques of agriculture and handicraft production were too rudimentary to produce enough goods to supply a truly national market. Communication among the provinces was still poor. Each locality therefore was almost totally self-sufficient. Only a few agricultural and handicraft products comprised regional commerce. The economy of each locality remained for the most part autarchic. Vietnam was a monarchy with a mandarin bureaucracy capping an agglomeration of rural villages.

Village life was lively and cohesive, however. The main occupation was growing rice in irrigated fields. Collective organization of agricultural waterworks, plus clusters of houses on small hillocks that rose like islands amid the flooded rice fields, made for stable, solidly organized rural communities. A farm isolated in the middle of a field has always been the exception in Vietnam.

The village paid taxes to the royal administration and supplied it with men for military service and public works. It held court for all but serious crimes and property disputes, which were tried in the mandarin courts. Each village assessed its own taxes and conscripted its own men for military duty and *corvée* labor. Each village was responsible for all civil litigation, the cult of the village guardian spirit or god, and the maintenance of order. The village was administered by a council of notables and a mayor, who were elected, in principle, by all the residents of the village.

Another important function of village administration was the periodical distribution of village-owned landholdings, which were supposed to be shared among all the citizens. Sometimes this land amounted to as much as 25 percent of the arable land. Within a village, residents descending from a common ancestor composed a clan, sometimes numbering several hundred people. Each family within a clan assembled in the temple of the ancestors to worship the dead. Clan representatives protected the interests of their members before the village administration.

Collective life was vibrant in these villages, which often counted several thousand members. Agricultural work, religious ceremonies, and family gatherings took place one after the other. Elections were held, and people plotted for positions as notables. Several types of organizations existed in the villages, such as associations for mutual assistance, gambling, loans, etc.

On the cultural and ideological level, the one person who could be singled out as a leader of this collective life was the Confucian scholar. The thousands of unsuccessful candidates for the mandarin examinations who returned to their villages were no better off than before, but because they had studied for so many years they did not want to plow a field or hammer a nail, let alone start a business. And so, the royal administration exempted them from all *corvées*, with the result that they could remain scholars for the rest of their lives. But they still had to make a living. Sometimes income from family lands was sufficient; often a wife spun or wove or maintained a small business to enable her husband to continue his studies until the next examination. The examinations were given only once every three years. Thus, scholars 50 or 60 years old would take the same tests as the 18-year-olds. Tens of thousands of scholars lived like this throughout the country, studying the classic texts over and over again and never giving up hope that they would be able to pass the exams one day.

While waiting for that fateful day, the scholars became teachers, masters of ceremonies, and public scribes. They drew up deeds, requests to mandarins, and summonses. They also kept the tax and civil records of the village. Some of them, having studied medical treatises, visited the sick and prescribed and sold medicines. Others, knowledgeable in astrology or geomancy, drew up horoscopes and advised people on how to position their houses or where to place their ancestral tombs—prime factors in the prosperity of the family or clan. Singing contests between boys and girls from neighboring villages were often held, with a scholar coaching each group of singers. Semi-professional theatrical troupes frequently gave *cheo* plays in the villages. In folk songs as well as in the *cheo* plays, peasant themes and language were combined with the literary technique of the scholars.

The most honored profession was that of school teacher. In every village there was always a rich family or clan which hired a teacher for its children. Often the temple of ancestors served as the schoolroom. Clan children learned how to read, write and recite classical texts by heart, and the most advanced learned how to write poems and essays on themes of Confucian doctrine in preparation for the examinations. The state played no part whatsoever in financing or appointing teachers. This was left entirely to private initiative. Mandarins responsible for education controlled only the number and academic level of students wishing to take the competitive exams. Because studying was highly esteemed, and because of widespread obsession with the mandarin examinations, there were schools everywhere. Every family, no matter how poor, did everything it could to send its children (at least the boys) to school if only to learn "a few letters." It was rare to find a totally illiterate person. When a child showed aptitude, the family would make great sacrifices to enable him to continue his studies. Clan members frequently shared the cost to some extent. To have a mandarin in the clan was the highest honor.

The system of one teacher to each class was universal. While younger children in one corner would falteringly recite couplets of a few ideograms containing the basis of traditional morality, the teacher would be commenting on some extremely difficult text to the men, who were sometimes very old, in preparation for the great examinations. The number of students in a class depended essentially on the fame of the teacher. Some teachers attracted students from distant provinces; hundreds of the best minds in the country would sometimes gather around them. When these venerable teachers made their commentaries on the texts, or had their disciples read their best compositions in front of hundreds of people of all ages, the meeting was more like an academic convocation than a class. The beautiful compositions and poems written in these schools circulated from one end of the country to the other, drawing impassioned comments. The great scholars enjoyed a nationwide reputation.

The law ruled, mandarins administered, and the village scholar, living close to the people, educated and advised them daily. Moral order depended on this large brotherhood of scholars, which gathered together by the thousands in the administrative centers of the country for each competitive examination. Mandarins and scholars were trained by the same books and the same teachers. Yet while the former enclosed themselves in their mandarin residences, the latter continued to live among the people, among the village peasants.

Humanism, Morality and Ritual

From the tenth to the fourteenth century, Confucian scholars and mandarins had to struggle together to eliminate Buddhism from its position of ideological leadership in the country. Buddhism affirmed the vanity (and even the un-reality) of the things of this world, preached renunciation, and directed people's minds toward supernatural hopes. Confucianism taught that man is above all a social being, bound by social obligations. The duties which Confucian doctrine assigned to everyone were service to the king, honoring one's parents, remaining faithful to one's spouse until death, managing family affairs well, participating in the administration of the country, and helping to maintain peace in the world. The basic preoccupation of every man "from the Emperor, Son of Heaven, to the last common man" was to mold and perfect himself so that he could assume those duties.

We must not forget that Confucius lived in the sixth century B.C., a time when men believed they were obliged to pay homage to gods and spirits rather than to men. Among people for whom supernatural life was as real as or more real than life in this world, Confucius displayed a great deal of courage in answering questions about the spirits and death as he did:

"If you don't know how to serve men, why worry about serving the gods?

"If you don't know how to live, why wonder about death?"

Commenting on these lines, Tseng-tzu, one of Confucius' disciples, added, "If one knows the way *(tao)* to live, one also knows the way to die. To serve men with all one's heart is to serve the gods as well." Note that in Chinese philosophy the word *tao* sometimes meant the ultimate truth, the fundamental law which ruled the universe; at other times it meant an essential rule of life for men. This overlapping of cosmic order and human order is one of the characteristics of Chinese thought.

Doctrines flourished in Confucius' time. Philosophers rubbed elbows with magicians; sophists vied with faith healers for the public square. But Confucius calmly stated:

> I never speak of mysteries and do miracles in order to leave a name to posterity . . . The gods should certainly be revered, but kept at a distance . . . The way is not beyond man; he who creates a way outside of man cannot make it a true way. A good man is content with changing man, and that is enough for him. . . . I am not someone who has received special enlightenment, I am merely a man who has studied a great deal and ceaselessly tried to teach others.

Prayers, sacraments, invocations to a god—none of these exists in Confucianism. It is understandable that Voltaire was attracted by this doctrine.

Thus, Vietnamese scholars from the tenth to the fourteenth century waged a battle against Buddhist beliefs. They were not, however, simply opposed to the beliefs themselves but also to the position assigned to those beliefs by state and society. The historian, Le Van Huu, wrote in the twelfth century:

> Scarcely two years after his coronation, although the ancestral temples of the dynasty hadn't yet been built, and the foundations of the state had not yet been consolidated, the first Ly king had already built eight pagodas in the district of Thien

Duc, restored several others in various provinces, and maintained more than a thousand bonzes in the capital city. What a waste of rice and labor! These things didn't come from heaven, and the gods didn't do the work that had to be done. So is this not sucking the blood and sweat of the people? Is sucking the blood and sweat of the people really such a blessing? Because the king who founded the Ly dynasty acted in this way, his successors, too, built pagodas with towers reaching to the sky. Buddha's residences outstripped royal palaces in magnificence. Subjects followed suit. Many went so far as to destroy their possessions and abandon their families. Half of the population became bonzes. Pagodas could be seen everywhere. Isn't that the origin of our troubles?

After the war against Champa in 1128, this same scholar wrote:

Alas! To elaborate strategy and tactics in the seclusion of tents, and to fight heroically thousands of leagues from home, is this not how generals prove their valor? But at home the king goes to the pagoda to give thanks to Buddha, attributing to him the glories of victory, while he has not a single word of praise for his deserving officers or encouragement for his brave soldiers.

We also have the following texts of Le Quat and Truong Han Sieu dating from the same time. Le Quat wrote:

Why have the fear of Buddha's maledictions and the need to implore his mercy become so deeply embedded in people's minds? Royal princes and common folk worship Buddha and squander their wealth on the pagodas. They are as happy as if they had received a written guarantee for the next world. People have faith in Buddhism and drift along with the tide without being ordered to do so, whether they live in the capital or in the most remote village. Wherever you see a house, you can be sure a pagoda is not far away. As soon as one pagoda collapses, another is built. Bells, drums, pagodas and towers are the center of the activities of half the population.

Considering the present state of Buddhism in Vietnam,

we can appreciate after reading these texts to what extent Buddhism was suppressed by Confucianism.

Truong Han Sieu was even more virulent than Le Quat:

> The ideal of Buddhist asceticism is completely negated by some Buddhist scoundrels whose sole interest is to corner the market on monasteries, all the large gardens with beautiful guilded mansions, attended by numerous servants. While they immerse themselves in the riches of this world, their pagodas occupy the most favorable spots in the country. Thousands of people become monks for free meals and for free clothing woven by others. Monks dupe the people, undermine morality, and waste people's resources. But they are everywhere and wherever they go, they are followed by huge crowds of the faithful, although most of them are little better than bandits.

Such vigorous attacks against the clergy would be voiced in the West only after several centuries. Vietnam was secularized in the fifteenth century. Refusing to nourish hope for an afterworld, the Confucian concentrated his efforts on purely human tasks such as studying, improving himself, and fulfilling his social obligations. To appreciate the full value of Confucian teaching, one should try to imagine what life was like in 500 B.C., when Confucianism first appeared and stated that man's efforts to perfect himself were more important than rendering homage to the gods.

The importance of learning is still engrained in Confucian peoples. The worthy person is one with an education, laden with diplomas. Knights, samurai or swashbucklers have never been held in great esteem in Vietnam. The civil mandarin bureaucracy always predominated over the military in the state apparatus. "I long for the brush and desk of the scholar, and not for lush rice fields and fish-filled ponds," sang Vietnamese girls.

Nevertheless, Confucian education aimed less at imparting knowledge than at inculcating an ethic, giving rules to live by and furnishing principles of conduct. From the first day of their schooling, six-year-olds had to recite:

"From birth, man is good by nature.

"Unpolished jade is worthless.

"Without study, man cannot know the principle of things . . . "

First the child, then the young man, then the mature adult, would recite and fashion commentaries on particular sentences and on the classic texts, for years and years, in order to learn how to honor his parents, how to behave toward his brothers and sisters, how to serve his king and how to conduct himself in all situations in life. History was studied at length to find examples of behavior, not to understand the unfolding of events or the development of societies. It hardly mattered that Chinese, not Vietnamese, history was being studied. Becuase it was richer, written Chinese history offered more material containing examples of proper attitudes and behavior and the moral doctrine of the Teacher.

Confucian phrases became deeply engraved in the mind of the student. He not only had an intellectual attachment to these sayings but also became imbued, through a process of incessant repetition, with all the principles and rules of life. Classical Chinese was written extremely succinctly; transitional words, conjunctions and prepositions were eliminated, and a sentence consisted of only a few nouns, verbs and adjectives, which were monosyllabic and very easy to memorize. It should be noted that Chinese (like Vietnamese) is a language in which syllables are pronounced with different tones. Therefore, the combination of the various tones of different words in a sentence creates a certain melody which is greatly appreciated by literary people. Approaching a Confucian school from a distance, one could hear the students chanting their texts rather than reading them. Their voices would rise and fall along with the tones of the words and the rhythm of the phrases and sentences. It could have been a choir rehearsal. In China as in Vietnam, a beautiful text is always one with a fine musical quality when read aloud. The ideographic writing also adds to the aesthetic appeal of the texts; each ideograph is a design with its own special architecture, and a well-written text is a veritable painting.

A cultured man had to have a beautiful handwriting. When a Confucian sentence is translated into a Western language like French, with its "who," "what," "therefore," "that's why" and "because," only the intellectual aspect of the text is being translated. The striking emotions, the music, and the pictures disappear. It is therefore difficult to understand the power these texts had over those who learned them. For example, when the proverb on how to study and improve oneself is translated into English, the translation simply causes a person to reflect:

"Study the way the worker fashions and works stone;

"Perfect yourself as the artisan rubs and polishes jade."

But the person reciting this in Chinese or Vietnamese, or writing it in ideographs, derives a musical and a visual enjoyment not conveyed in the translation. The maxim not only is assimilated intellectually but also becomes an integral part of the student's sensitivity. Study becomes inseparable from the work of oneself on oneself, work which must be done every day at every moment. One of Confucius' disciples said:

"Every day, three times a day, I examine myself to see whether I may have failed to serve others, failed to keep my word to my friends, or forgotten to apply the principles I have been taught."

This long path to wisdom is defined as follows in the *Great Learning (Ta-hsüeh)*:

> Investigate things closely in order to gain knowledge. Gain knowledge in order to strengthen the sincerity of your thoughts, and thus ensure the rectification of your heart. Ensure the rectification of your heart in order to perfect yourself. Having done your work on yourself well, you can put your family in order. Having managed your family well, you may participate in administering the country. Having administered your country well, you can contribute to keeping peace in the world.

The plan is not lacking in greatness. Confucius was among the first philosophers to concentrate the entire attention of men on purely human problems. He was the first humanist, in the fullest sense of the term. In rereading the *Analects (Lun-yü)*, conversations of Confucius recorded by disciples, one can see that almost alll their talks revolved around the word "humanity" (*jen*). The Confucians did not limit the virtue of humanity to love of one's neighbor; it was very difficult to discern its limits because it was the supreme virtue, the one that makes man the most human he can possibly be. If the essential components absolutely had to be defined, they could be reduced to four principles:

—tolerance toward others (do not do to others what you would not have them do to you);

—knowledge, which enables you to have the right attitude in all situations of life;

—courage to fulfill your obligations;

—behavior in accordance with the rituals.

Each word, each gesture, of a worthy person had to be in accordance with the rituals; this is the essence of Confucian doctrine. There are rituals for honoring one's parents, for married life, for relationships between brothers and sisters and among friends, for behavior toward superiors or inferiors. There are rituals to express joy, anger and mourning. There are rituals for eating and even for sleeping (the worthy man does not stretch himself out like a plank of wood). A worthy man is watchful of his words, his gestures, his dress; he expresses his feelings according to the situation and circumstance. A "barbarian" is someone who does not know the rituals, who does not control himself and his feelings. I shall always remember my father using that epithet. For him it was the ultimate insult. My father would ruthlessly punish any child he heard swearing. We would be subject to the greatest reproach if we happened to say the clock was "dead" instead of saying it had stopped. Death is a bad word, unworthy of being uttered by worthy men. Furthermore, the Vietnamese language uses different words for "I" or "me," based on whether one is speaking to one's equals, superiors or inferiors.

The word "ritual" has three senses—religious, social and moral. It also signifies ceremonies for worship as well as etiquette observed in social relationships and the worthy behavior each person owes to himself out of self-respect. A man must observe the rituals even when he is by himself. The observance of ritual dominates all individual and social life: in Confucian society one would not kiss other people, even children. The most beautiful of speeches would never be applauded. Private citizens, no matter how rich, do not have the right to build houses as large as the mandarins' mansions. People were excessively fussy about all matters of hierarchy, etiquette and the prerogatives accorded to each social stratum.

We can now draw a portrait of the Confucian man. He studied a great deal, but his education was somewhat restricted for he was interested only in the "humanities" and was totally indifferent to anything concerning nature. He was profoundly moral, imbued with principles he sincerely believed in. He was a social being, unable to imagine that man could divest himself of his social obligations. He was ceremonious, respectful of social conventions, intolerant of nonchalance in gestures, speech or dress.

For Confucians, training in the virtue of humanity began with filial piety. "Children have to take on all the difficult tasks" in order to sweeten and beautify the lives of their parents. From their first classes, children learned to follow the example of the little boys who slept naked next to their parents in order to attract all the mosquitoes to their own little bodies, or the children who warmed their parents' bed with their own body heat before their parents retired each evening. It would be unthinkable in Vietnam for well-to-do children to allow their parents to live out their lives in an old-age home. When I first arrived in France, the scene that surprised me most was a girl amusing herself by teasing her father about his bald head.

Confucianism of the Mandarins and Confucianism of the People

We have already spoken of the scholar Nguyen Trai, a writer, strategist and statesman who helped the peasant landowner Le Loi found the Le dynasty in the fifteenth century. He was a humanist in the fullest sense. The peasant landowning class which came to power eliminated the great feudal families, abolished serfdom and took responsibility for defending national independence. Confucianism became the ideology of the new society. In 1428, when Nguyen Trai had to draw up an edict for the king announcing to the people that victory over the foreign invader had been won and national independence restored, he wrote a text that bristled with national pride and the pride of those conscious of creating a new era:

> Acting in the name of Heaven, the Emperor decrees:
> Peace for the people, that is the unshakeable foundation for the
>   virtues of Humanity and Justice.
> We have raised the banner to chase away the aggressor,
> Our Fatherland, home of an age-old civilization . . .

A few years later, in the name of the first Le king, Nguyen Trai wrote the following advice for the crown prince:

> I have come out of brambles and thorns, paid with my skin to chase the aggressors. I have worn a coat of armor and slept in fields. I have known peril and danger, braved sabers and swords and swept aside clouds and hurricanes to found the Empire at the price of innumerable difficulties. You who, because of my work, will succeed me, must not seek pleasure. Apply yourself, make every effort to follow all the rules that will enable you to safeguard the national patrimony and command the army. Follow every principle that teaches you how to discipline yourself and govern your country...
>
> Keep harmonious relations with your neighbors and be cordial to them. Remember to be generous to the people. Do not

bestow rewards merely out of personal inclination. Do not unjustly penalize someone out of anger. Do not pursue the wealth of a lavish life; keep away from beautiful women to avoid debauchery.

Whether it be to promote a talented man, to receive criticism, to develop policy, or merely to pronounce a single word or make a single gesture, keep the rule of the Golden Mean. Follow the classical principles, and you will answer the will of Heaven and satisfy the rituals. To hold in esteem those who possess the virtue of humanity is to be assured of the consent of the people who bear the throne, like the ocean which carries the ship but can also overturn it. To help men of virtue is to attract the protection of Heaven to yourself—and the will of Heaven is still so difficult to fathom and foresee . . .

Nguyen Trai drew this ethic of the model prince directly from Confucian doctrine. Confucian humanism was above all political. If Confucius and his disciples tried throughout their lives to define the virtue of humanity in all aspects, they did so less in order to teach it generally than to inculcate it specifically into the princes of their time. Confucius was above all a man who sought the best formula for government. He lived in a time of profound social upheavals; the slave-holding principalities of ancient China were giving way to large kingdoms. This process continued for centuries, ending with the unification of China under the authority of a feudal monarch. There were two opposing schools on matters of politics: the "legalists," who advised recasting the edicts and institutions and having government according to law; and the Confucians who extolled government according to ethics and ritual. The Ch'in and Han dynasties, which had liquidated the principalities and kingdoms in order to unify China under their authority, took their ideas from the legalists during their periods of conquest and while they made necessary changes. Once their empires were founded, however, and the new society was consolidated and the mandarin bureaucracy in place, Confucianism was put in a position of honor. This was because on the level of politics, Confucianism was essentially conservative. It ignored questions of law and social examination, systematically refusing any change. Moralism in politics is basically conservative. Directing people's thoughts to moral perfection in order to improve society without wishing to bring institutions into question has always been the policy of those who feared social upheavals. No wonder Camus was attracted by Confucianism.

Nevertheless, Confucianism did contribute one major idea: that the prince and his dignitaries—that is to say, the politicians in power— must have exemplary moral behavior. In Confucian society, the immorality of the rulers has always provided revolutionaries with their best arguments.

In fact, Confucianism was more than just conservative; it turned squarely toward the past. The ultimate concern of Confucius was to preserve the rituals of the "former kings." The Chinese monarchy and later the Vietnamese throne found in ritualism the best means to guarantee the stability of the imperial state.

Strict moral rules and precise rituals constituted the best methods of government for Confucians. Even filial piety served the function of maintaining social order. One of Confucius' eminent disciples said, "I know of almost no man filled with filial piety who challenges authority."

Nonetheless, it was necessary to justify these moral rules and rituals and attribute some basis to them. Let us reread the texts by Nguyen Trai. As in all the Confucian texts that discuss politics and ethics, we can find a symmetrical balance between two words: heaven and people. Where does the power of the state come from? Who gives the king his power: heaven or the people? For centuries, Confucian thought continually vacillated between these two poles on the political and social levels. Similarly, on the philosophical level, it hesitated between two theses: the primacy of *ly* (the principle of objects) and the primacy of *khi* (the life-breath and substance of things). Naturally, those who affirmed the priority of *ly* tended to believe in the celestial origin of royal power, while those who favored *khi* were more likely to attribute the origin of royal power to the people.

This was not a mere ideological struggle. Profound social forces, locked in ancient conflict, took shape behind these academic debates. Although the class of landowning peasants had abolished serfdom, agricultural exploitation remained severe and the mandarin administration heavy-handed. The majority of the peasants still owned no land. They ceaselessly demanded an equitable distribution of village land, lowering of rents, interest rates and taxes, fewer *corvées*, and especially the right to own land. Since they frequently assembled to work on agricultural water projects, this landless peasantry was a constant threat to the social order, which rested on the trilogy of land, mandarin bureaucracy and absolute monarchy. Though the Confucian mandarins affected disdain for laws in theory, they enacted rather strict legislation in reality. Although they despised the military, they mercilessly repressed any peasant uprisings. The foundations of traditional society were also undermined by the class of craftsmen and merchants, which was trying to expand the market economy. The mandarins suppressed trade and opposed technical and scientific progress. Under these conditions, the humanism of the peasant landowner class could not fully develop.

Since heaven was always envisioned in the image of earthly society, as soon as there was a king to rule on earth, there had to be an Emperor of Heaven as well. Confucius made no allowances for a personal, incarnate God who could always be counted on to intervene in people's lives. But Confucius still did not divest himself completely of the idea of a supreme spiritual principle that governed the world. The meaning of the words *tao* and heaven remained ambiguous in Confucian texts; it was unclear whether these words signified a principle or a person who governed the world.

Those ideologues who favored absolute monarchy and social conservatism argued purely and simply that the celestial Emperor had given the earthly Emperor a mandate to rule in his name. The king became the concrete link between heaven, earth and man. He not only ruled over men, but accorded titles to the guardian spirits as well. The rituals and moral rules were therefore considered to be heavenly in origin. They had to be observed scrupulously under penalty of punishment from on high. The Ministry of Rites made sure that the configuration of the stars was observed, drew up the calendar, accorded titles to guardian spirits, gave diplomas to virtuous people, regulated ceremonies of the court at all great social occasions, and was in charge of public education. There was no Ministry of Education under the monarchy, despite the fact that mandarins were recruited by competitive examination.

The cult of the Emperor was the apex of the structure of the mandarins' doctrine. Whenever the Son of Heaven passed through the streets, no one had the right to look at him. In Vietnam, as in China, people's names were chosen from among common words. The Emperor's name had to be eliminated from any texts; heaven help the poor candidate who forgot and used the word in any composition! Not only would he fail the examination, but he would be condemned as well. In order to enforce this rule, the mandarin bureaucracy would carefully maintain the cult of the Emperor and the customary rites. In principle, the opportunity to become a mandarin was open to all. In an agrarian society, however, where commerce and industry did not amount to much, social mobility was very restricted. Each person tried to push himself ahead, but very few managed to break through.

The ritualism of Confucian doctrine, together with this social immobility, gave rise to an acute sensitivity to social hierarchy. Every little rank, honorific title or place on the social scale was bitterly disputed. Each person tried to "save face." The king and mandarins would lash out against any lack of respect due them. School teachers would not hesitate to whip their students for the slightest misdemeanor. The whole village would gossip whenever a person arranged a funeral for his parents that may have been too modest. The peasant began as a "*bach dinh*" and at this level could be taxed and arbitrarily forced to join *corvées*, having no rights whatsoever. Then, depending on his moral and financial standing, he became *"seo," "chau," "nhieu,"* and so on. In this way he would gradually climb the grades of the village hierarchy in the same way that the mandarin would get closer and closer to the imperial court. Each person jealously guarded the prerogatives he had acquired. After the ceremonies honoring the village guardian spirit, the head, beak and crown of the sacrificial rooster had to be set aside for the highest ranking notables. Heaven help anyone else who took a piece for himself! Notables were known to commit crimes just to get the crown of a rooster.

Filial piety became a bridle on any initiative. Children were forbidden to travel while their parents were still alive. Honoring one's parents meant, above all, doing as they did, living like them, and carrying out their traditions of living and thinking.

Little by little, studying became pure scholasticism. Texts had to be learned by heart, and commentaries had to be made in a spirit of complete orthodoxy. Not a single comma could be changed in the "sacred" texts.

The free peasant became a landowner; the mandarin statesman became a member of the court; the humanist scholar became nothing more than a keeper of rituals. A century after Nguyen Trai, the great minds such as Nguyen Binh Khiem no longer had the courage to engage in public life. Peasant revolts shook the monarchy, and the mandarinate had basically become an instrument of repression. Still, the hermit Nguyen Binh Khiem remained deeply imbued with Confucianism. He could not help giving advice to the ruling princes. As a great scholar, he kept in close contact with hundreds of other scholars scattered throughout the country, a network which was the best means of taking the pulse of public opinion.

The ordinary scholar, that is to say the majority of them, consciously or unconsciously defended the traditional regime (just like intellectuals of all times). The most perceptive scholars, however, living among the people, could not help but see the other side of the coin. As long as there were cycles of "order and prosperity" in traditional society, both mandarins and scholars shared a veneration of the Emperor and continued to do commentaries on the classical texts. But, come a catastrophic flood, a prolonged dry spell, or the reign of a debauched king, and the impoverished and exasperated peasants would revolt. Some village scholars would then take up leadership of a rebel movement in the name of Confucian humanism and ethics in an attempt to overturn the reigning monarchy. At that point, the mandarins would invoke the name of Confucius when they called on the royal army to put down the revolt of the "insurgents." Students of the same teacher, from the same school, would sometimes be pitted against each other.

To the scholars who revolted or just stayed close to the peasants whom they advised from day to day, the idea that the Emperor was the Son of Heaven was pure fiction. The popular saying, "He who wins becomes Emperor, he who loses becomes an outlaw," reflected the reality of things far more truthfully. In contrast to the official rites, a popular type of common sense developed and found a valuable ally in the non-conformist scholar. Popular sayings and proverbs could easily be found as retort to each classical sentence. The popular theater, *cheo*, was basically satirical and always characterized the mandarins and notables in a bad light. The monarchy and mandarin bureaucracy adopted classical literary Chinese as the official language. The scholar who was close to the people created *nom* writing in order to transcribe his work into the ordinary language. When the Tay Son popular movement won, *nom* was adopted as the official language. After the Nguyen dynasty suppressed the Tay Son, classical Chinese was reestablished as the official language.

Thus, for centuries there were two streams of Confucian thought. Everyone revered the Great Master and no one dared attack his doctrine, yet each school of thought interpreted the texts as it pleased. Paul Mus' book on the sociology of Vietnam makes a serious mistake in presenting only the orthodox mandarin side of these traditional ideas and beliefs in Vietnam.[1]

Modern Scholars and Intellectuals

During the second half of the nineteenth century, Vietnam faced colonial aggression. The split between mandarins and scholars widened. The monarchy and mandarins hurried to make a pact with the enemy because the throne and mandarins' ranks were more important to them than national independence. Yet, despite the court's appeals to "remain calm," scholars in the villages, confident of support from the people, and heir to many centuries of national struggle, proceeded to mobilize the peasants and organize the resistance. Scholars from North to South became warriors, leading students and peasants from their provinces to battle over a 20-year period. If captured, they died courageously, either under torture or at gunpoint. But they lacked modern weapons and, more significantly, a political doctrine adapted to the new times, so they succumbed one after another. Yet the patriotic scholars saved the honor of Confucianism at the time when it was disappearing from the stage of Vietnamese history. Vietnam approached the twentieth century with a battle-weary Confucianism. Subsequent attempts at revival would prove nothing more than a reactionary charade. (The Vichy regime, for instance, tried to give new life to Confucianism in Indochina.)

The defeat of the scholars in the face of the colonial aggressor resulted not only from inferior weapons. Ideological deficiencies were just as blatantly a cause. Even popular Confucianism had limits imposed on it by the nature of its origin and by its characteristics as a peasant ideology.

The Vietnamese bourgeoisie was never able to become a powerful class because its development was thwarted by the

[1]Paul Mus, *Viet Nam: Sociologie d'une Guerre* (Paris: Editions du Seuil, 1952)—*Ed.*

mandarins. The numerous revolts that marked Vietnamese history were all peasant movements. These peasants and the scholars who led them saw the outcome of their movements only in terms of the coronation of a new king who would possess the humanity and justice required by Confucian doctrine. As did Mencius, they thought that the people were most important. But, also in accordance with Mencius, they thought that those who worked with their hands had to be governed, while those who worked with their heads should do the governing. It could never be reversed, they felt. The king and the mandarins who governed the people were to be considered mothers and fathers. The notion of democracy was completely foreign to the people who fought only to replace an "inhumane" king with a "humane" one, or an "illegitimate" king with a "legitimate" prince. Patriotic scholars did not consider institutional changes necessary for adaptation to a new world. They fought against modern colonialism just as their ancestors had fought against the feudal Chinese invader, with the same methods and the same ideas.

Furthermore, the scholars could not comprehend modern science because they were completely oblivious to the problems of production. They disdained manual work and honored exercises of the mind alone. The scholar with unusually long fingernails "incapable of catching a chicken" (a popular Vietnamese expression) was not a mere metaphor. The country could not count on him to modernize the means of production.

The generations after 1900 no longer wanted to die for a degenerate monarchy or for Confucius. The bloody defeats inflicted by a colonial aggressor armed with modern weapons, the Japanese victory over the tsarist army in 1905, and the reading of the works of Jean-Jacques Rousseau and Montesquieu shocked open-minded scholars and the country as a whole. Two new concepts, completely foreign to Confucianism, burst into Vietnam: science and democracy. People began to see solutions outside the ruts of the past.

For many scholars, the discovery that it was possible to have a regime other than a monarchy and that people could and should participate in politics came as a distinct revelations. Machines and scientific study were also revelations. True, scholars sequestered in their villages had been raised to study medicine and geomancy. But since Taoism was the basis of their thought, they were unable to distinguish between science and magic. Astronomy was confused with astrology, geography and geology with geomancy, and even medicine, which in certain fields had led to remarkable results, could not divest itself of magical practices.

But for a long time to come, the ideas of science and democracy would be merely sparks in the night, incapable of igniting an entire country. From 1905 to 1930, Vietnam seemed drowsy and resigned to accepting colonial domination. New generations of intellectuals set themselves the task of studying the science and democracy of the West, but none of them, as knowledgeable as they may have been, could have led the country in an uprising like the one the great scholars led at the end of the nineteenth century. We (I use the word "we" because the author of these lines is one of those intellectuals who graduated from the University of Hanoi or returned home from France during the colonial period) learned what the Confucian scholars lacked: physics, algebra, biology, electoral politics, republican constitutions. But when we compared ourselves with the traditional scholars, whom we still saw on a regular basis, we definitely felt they had something we lacked.

Their knowledge was relatively limited, but they were "men," they were the "bamboo trees" which remained tall, "pines" that withstood the adversities of winter. As for ourselves, we were mere "deposits of knowledge," reeds that bent under the slightest breeze, unreliable in times of difficulty. With their deeply-rooted moral convictions, the scholars had principles to which they adhered. The validity of these principles could be debated, but their existence was certain, since these men never acted against their convictions.

Ethics was the very basis of their education.

Our own training was different. In high school and at the university, we paid special attention to chemistry, trigonometry and geography courses. When it was time for ethics, we secretly read novels or played naval battles. The scholars never knew what a scientist was, whereas we never knew what a worthy man was. And most of us, although not all, were like clay when it came to standing up against opposing forces that played with us at will.

The several thousand intellectuals who were trained in the universities of France or Hanoi in the colonial period lived like mandarins of the past, apart from the people. We were city dwellers in a country that was still 95 percent rural. But when the fraternity of scholars formulated a program in the old days, the entire country knew about it because the scholars were in daily contact with the peasants. We, on the other hand, were submerged in the cities in the middle of our country without antenna or compass.

We did not even become mandarins under the new regime, since foreigners ruled the country. The scholars saw themselves as descendants of past Vietnamese rulers and leaders who had led the people in the age-old national struggle. The best of these scholars had a sense of pride and confidence in themselves which we lacked. The people reverently recited the names of the scholars who succumbed during the struggle against the French colonial regime, defying torture and the execution squad. These men preferred jail to honors and riches, in line with the famous quotation from Mencius:

> To dwell in the broad house which is the world,
> To stand upright, to travel the main highway . . .
> To be uncorrupted by riches and honors,
> To remain firm when poor and in low estate,
> To be unflinching even when threatened with force—
> This is to be a mighty man.[2]

[2]Adapted from James R. Ware, trans., *The Sayings of Confucius*

Our generation had another handicap. We had done all our studying in French, so very few of us knew how to write correctly in our native Vietnamese. We were voiceless before our own people, cut off from our national heritage.

Modern ideas of science and democracy filled our minds, but we were powerless when it came to striking down the colonial regime, destroying the country's feudal structure, and replacing it with a democratic system and a scientific mode of production. These tasks were too heavy for our frail shoulders to bear. Our social base, the Vietnamese bourgeoisie, was far too fragile. All it could do was vegetate in the shadow of colonial domination. We were at a loss to know where to begin; we felt totally disarmed in the face of Western imperialism. Intellectuals who graduated from the university during the colonial period were thus unable to play the same role the Confucian scholars had played in the time of Nguyen Trai.

Confucians and Marxists

From 1930, when the Communist Party of Indochina was founded, leadership of the national struggle and the role of pioneers in a new society passed to Marxist cadres. Only 15 years after it was founded, the Party established the first independent government in Vietnam since the colonial conquest. A war of national liberation followed, lasted nine years, and led to the building of socialist in the northern part of the country.

The first Marxist cadres were, for the most part, "petty intellectuals" who had been forced to end their studies before taking their baccalaureate exams and who worked as clerks in the colonial administration, factories and plantations. Others were village teachers, often at private schools, just like the scholars of old. As "pencil-holding coolies," they shared with the workers and poor peasants their misery, their

(New York, 1960), p. 90.—*Ed.*

fear of unemployment, and their humiliations. Benefiting from the prestige held by educated men in a country with a strong Confucian tradition, the cadres naturally assumed the role of adviser to the people with whom they rubbed shoulders every day. Marxism thus came to Vietnam not as just another doctrine, but as an instrument of liberation after the Confucian scholars had failed to liberate the country and the efforts of the bourgeois intellectuals against the colonial and feudal regimes had proved feeble and without promise. In replacing Confucianism, Marxism gave the country a political and social doctrine that enabled it to solve practical problems. Marxism confronted Confucianism in the field of historical development, not in the midst of academic debates. Old fashioned mandarins and notables who remained in the service of colonialism fought Marxism bitterly; they fully realized that the antiquated private agrarian system and feudal structure would not survive confrontation with peasants led by communist cadres.[3]

Marxist cadres continued the tradition of the old-time revolutionary scholars by sequestering themselves in the villages, teaching and organizing the peasants over a period of many long years, until the time of land reform and the establishment of agricultural cooperatives. By doing so, they raised peasant struggle to a much higher level, opening it up to entirely new perspectives. At the same time, they struck a mortal blow at mandarinal Confucianism.

The great patriotic scholars Phan Boi Chau and Huynh Thuc Khang (to cite only the most famous) were attracted to the new doctrine as soon as it appeared in Vietnam. Unswerving enemies of the colonial regime, they felt a deep affinity with the new revolutionary cadres who were devoted body and soul to the national cause, as the scholars had been. Marxists and genuine Confucians shared more than common political goals. They were also related in the realm of

[3]Ngo Dinh Diem was one of the most zealous servants of the colonial regime during the repression which started in 1930.

thought, which facilitated rapprochement and sometimes a leap from one doctrine to the other. It was easier for a Confucian country than for a Muslim or Christian one to adopt Marxism, because Confucianism had not speculated throughout the centuries about the "other world." And Confucians had reacted more vigorously against Christianity than others, not only because Catholic missionaries were often the precursors of colonialism, but also because the concepts of divine grace, sacraments and God incarnate were foreign to Confucian thinking.

Marxism was not baffling to Confucians in that it concentrated man's thoughts on political and social problems. By defining man as the total of his social relationships, Marxism hardly came as a shock to the Confucian scholar who had always considered the highest aim of man to be the fulfillment of his social obligations. Although there was certainly a wide gap between the purely moral definition of social obligations in Confucianism and the scientific definition of social relationships in Marxism, both doctrines shared the same frame of reference and concerns. Bourgeois individualism, which puts personal interests ahead of those of society, and petty bourgeois anarchism, which allows no social discipline whatsoever, are alien to both Confucianism and Marxism. The Confucian man makes the transition from a traditional society to a socialist one. He is never actually hostile to the principle of collective discipline (as is the bourgeois intellectual) since he always sees social discipline as an indispensable part of the development of his own personality.

Marxist cadres also drew freely from the political morality of Confucians. The notion that leaders should exemplify high moral standards was deeply engrained in Confucian countries. Today's Marxists, while lending a different meaning to their actions, continue the tradition of famous scholars of former times. They still recite Confucian sayings: "Do not be corrupted by wealth," "Do not succumb in the face of adversity," and "Do not bow your head before demonstrations of force." Even Bernard Fall, a vigorous anti-communist author, acknowledged in his books on the Viet Minh the fact that Vietnamese communists adhered to a high moral standard. Fall cited the example of tax-collecting cadres who carried large amounts of money yet almost died of hunger trying to reach their destinations.

During the war of national liberation, a small text, modestly titled *Let's Change our Methods of Work*, was used as a handbook by the Party militants. Here are some typical passages from this pamphlet:

> It is not difficult for a cadre to become a real revolutionary if he wants to. Everything depends on him. If his sole interest is the Party, the country and his compatriots, he will become totally selfless, dedicated to serving the public good. In doing so, his personal faults will decrease and his virtues will become increasingly apparent each day. The revolutionary virtues are five in all: humanity, a sense of duty, knowledge, courage, and integrity.

> The virtue of humanity consists of loving deeply and wholeheartedly assisting one's comrades and compatriots. That is why the cadre who displays this virtue wages a resolute struggle against all those who would harm the Party and people. That is why he will not hesitate to be the first to endure hardship and the last to enjoy happiness. That is why he will not covet wealth and honor, nor fear hardship and suffering, nor be afraid to fight those in power.

> Those who want nothing are afraid of nothing and will always succeed in doing the right thing.

> Having a sense of duty means uprightness—not having ulterior motives, doing nothing unjust and having nothing to hide from the Party. It also means not being preoccupied by personal interests in conflict with those of the Party. Any task assigned by the Party, large or small, should be done conscientiously. When a certain matter is correct it must be carried out to the end. When something is right it must be expressed, no matter what. One should not be afraid to be criticized by others, and one should bear in mind everyone's interests when criticizing others.

> Since one's conscience is not clouded by personal interests,

clarity of purpose can be easily maintained. It becomes easier to reason and find the right way. One can judge men and investigate matters. Useful projects can be accomplished, while interests harmful to the Party can be avoided. For the sake of the just cause, people of value will be promoted while vigilance against crooks is maintained.

Having courage means carrying out what one believes is right. It means not being afraid to correct one's faults, to endure suffering, and to face hardship. It means not hesitating to reject honors and ill-gained wealth. If necessary, it means the sacrifice of one's life for the Party and country without qualm.

Having integrity means not coveting status or wealth, not seeking an easy life or becoming angered because of the actions of others. That is why one can be lucid and generous, and avoid self-degradation. Our only aim should be to study, work and make progress.

This is the essence of revolutionary morality. It is not a conservative morality. Rather, it is a new and great morality which does not aim at increasing individual prestige but serves only the interests of the Party, the nation and mankind.

A river cut off from its source will dry up and disappear. A tree severed from its roots will wither. A revolutionary lacking morality will never accomplish his goal of leading the people, no matter how talented he may be. Our aim is to liberate our people and humanity—what a great task this is! But if we ourselves are selfish, immoral, rootless, decadent, what can we accomplish?

Here is another example from a speech given by Ho Chi Minh in April, 1961 at the opening of the "rectification" campaign:

The cadres and members of the Party must maintain a high sense of responsibility to the Party and the masses, and must put themselves entirely in the service of the people. They must have true respect for the sovereignty of the people. They must be very careful lest they behave like "revolutionary mandarins," dictating from above. They must adopt the class outlook, rigorously follow the mass line, sincerely try to learn from the masses, resolutely rely on the masses, teach and mobilize them to apply the line and policy of the Party and the state. They must prove their sincerity and uprightness by not concealing their ignorance, weaknesses or errors. They must be modest, remain close to the masses and not be arrogant. They must take a realistic approach and not be governed by subjectivism. They must always put the well-being of the population above all. They must opt for the collective interests first and always be ready to be the first to suffer and the last to find happiness. These are the ethics of communism.

The above passages would not be out of place in an anthology of Confucian writings, and in them one can clearly perceive the political morality of Confucianism. These are not lessons in ethics such as would be given in high school or university, since they are policy guidelines for rectification campaigns. Political and ideological orders are sent down from the highest levels of the Party each time a new task of great importance arises, a new step has to be taken, or a new solution is needed during a crisis. Cadres meet to study political texts, give their opinions, and express approval or disapproval. Then they begin to evaluate the people's actions and the work that has been accomplished. They plan future tasks, compensations, praise and sanctions on the basis of political facts. They undertake criticism and self-criticism, which often result in intricate moral analysis.

In Vietnam, as in China, it could even be said that Confucianism has left its mark on some aspects of Marxist thought. Revolutionary morality in Confucian countries often is more influential than notions of the law of historical development. Since Marxism is both "explanation and edification," edification may often take precedence. Among the great family of Communist Parties, the Vietnamese and Chinese have particularly exhibited more of a moralistic tone than Communist Parties elsewhere, where the bourgeoisie has exercised ideological leadership over a long period of time. In those countries, bourgeois amorality has frequently influenced Marxist cadres, who tend to neglect the problems of personal ethics.

This moralism can sometimes lead to a sort of voluntarism, which considers no task impossible as long as the cadres are sufficiently dedicated. However, given the scientific character of Marxism, the risk of this happening is not serious.

This scientific nature represents the fundamental and definitive difference between Confucianism and Marxism. The most vivid example of a Confucian scholar who changed from one philosophy to the other is surely President Ho Chi Minh. His change was not easy or simple, the result of reading a couple of books or of solitary reflection. The type of Confucian who adopted Marxism would always be an activist who had campaigned for national independence, had suffered failure over the years, had spent time in prison, and had failed to reform the villages. His transition to Marxism stemmed from revolutionary practice, not from reading books. He reconstructed his entire thinking.

Technical backwardness, the lowest level of productive forces, made people consider historical evolution from just the moral angle. Ideological education and practical experience are necessary to make people aware of the problems of production. "Everything for production" was one of the orders given during the rectification campaign in 1961.

Consciously or not, the Confucian attaches moral values to heaven. Man ends up attaining this heaven by burying it deep inside himself. In the above-mentioned text of the *Great Learning (Ta-hsüeh)* we find: "Scrutinize things to find knowledge." In the classical interpretation taught in the schools, to scrutinize things meant to examine the depths of oneself. Through complete honesty with himself, the wise man attained a communion with heaven, and would then be able to act upon the cosmic order. Confucian texts were vague about whether the high moral standards required of rulers affected the people through the nature of the social collective or by means of this "mysterious correspondence" between the human order and the cosmic order.

Long years of colonial domination and much experience in revolutionary struggle were prerequisite to eliminating this cosmic subjectivism and to finding acceptance for the idea that human values originate in man's material existence.

Today, Marxism has replaced Confucianism as a doctrine of political and social action, and a new revolutionary ethic has replaced Confucian morality in Vietnam. Any attempt to revive Confucianism is useless. But, contrary to what pseudo-revolutionaries believe, Vietnamese Marxists consider Confucianism and the work of the scholars part of their national heritage, to be assimilated by the new society.

Boys rowing on Returned Sword Lake in central Hanoi. When Chinese troops invaded Vietnam in the early fifteenth century, Le Loi led a victorious popular resistance. Legend says that a huge turtle from this lake presented him with a sword, which he used to defeat the invaders. Afterwards, he returned the sword to the lake and built the pagoda in the background. The French put a statue of Liberté *on top of the pagoda, symbolizing their domination. However, this did not prevent modernizing scholar-patriots from holding public meetings there in 1907-08, until repressed by colonial police. With final liberation in 1954, the statue was replaced by the flag of the Democratic Republic of Vietnam. Later more than one American pilot found himself being fished out of Returned Sword Lake. Today, the lake retains all its symbolism and is a favorite place of relaxation as well. (photo by Ann Dockery, Liberation News Service)*

A traditional Vietnamese folk print depicting General Tran Hung Dao, leader of the successful thirteenth century struggle against the Mongols.

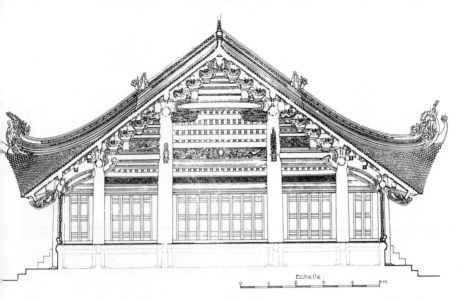

Two examples of traditional Confucian architecture. Above, the royal Temple of iterature in Hanoi. Below, the village meeting hall/temple of Dinh Bang, in Bac Ninh rovince.

Two alternatives for Vietnamese confucian scholars in the colonial period: brushing Tet, greetings, poems and votive offerings (above); or serving the French, getting land, and being "honored" with medals (left).

Fifteenth century commemorative tablet for top civil examination graduates. Located in the courtyard of the Temple of Literature, Hanoi.

Education under the French colonial regime. Observe who sits, who stands. By the 1930s there was one university with only about 600 students. Nguyen Khac Vien studied medicine there.

Peasants pulling plows after the French had killed their buffalo.

The August 1945 Revolution. The people overrun a French outpost near Ben Tre, southern Vietnam.

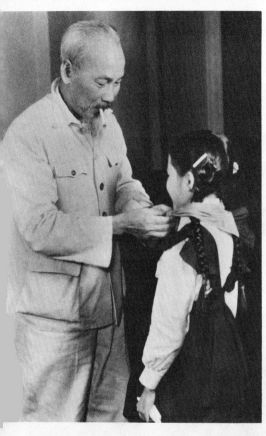

Ho Chi Minh presents a red scarf to Young Pioneer representative, 1960. He had received the scarf from international youth admirers. A Young Pioneer presents a scarf to President Ton Duc Thang (below), during a 1973 conference for the protection, care and education of children.

Ho Chi Minh encouraging members of an adult literacy class, 1956.

1962 campaign to improve and expand local medical facilities. Ho Chi Minh and Pham Ngoc Thach, Minister of Health, discuss progress with a leading medical team.

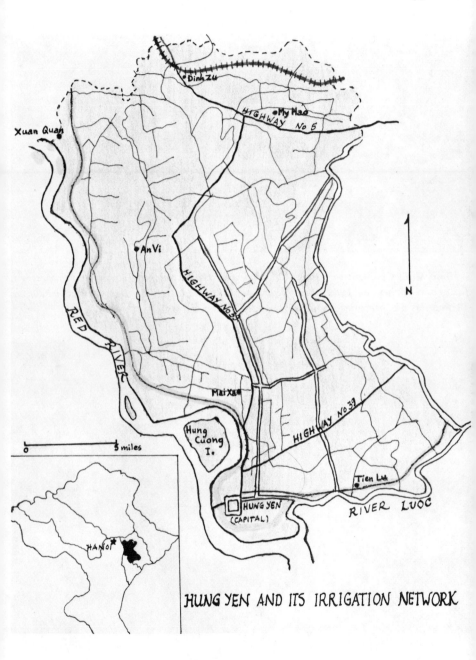

HUNG YEN AND ITS IRRIGATION NETWORK

Binh Minh Cooperative (Hung Yen province). Harvesting jute (above) and preparing it for export (below) in 1963. Binh Minh Coop is located in Khoai Chau district, which Dr. Vien writes was previously renowned mostly for its beggars.

Hong Thang Coop (Hung Yen). Water control is important to increasing rice yields and growing secondary crops.

Dike maintenance continues in Hung Yen (now part of Hai Hung province) in April 1974.

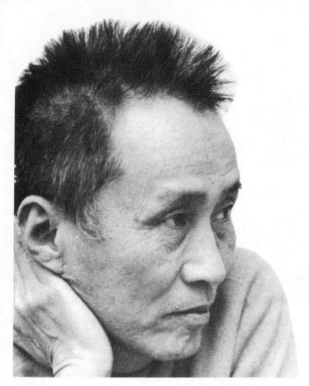

Dr. Nguyen Khac Vien.

Dr. Vien being interviewed by staff and friends of Jeune Afrique *February 1973.*

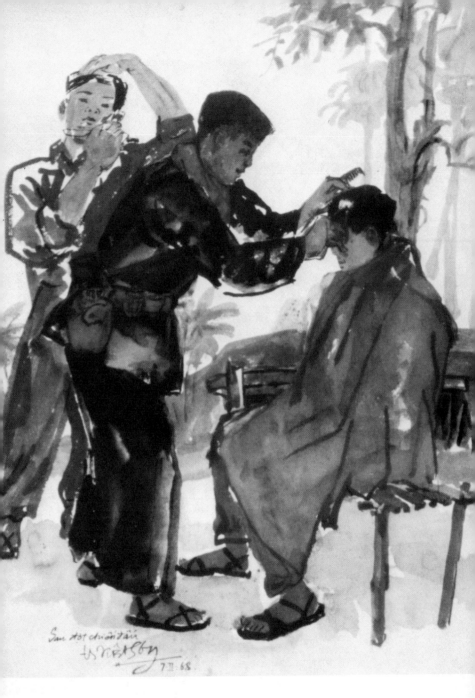

After a battle. 1968 watercolor by Viet Son.

Painting by Dang Van Phuc, ten-year-old student, of the shattered Long Bien Bridge in Hanoi and pontoons and ferry set up as alternative means of crossing the Red River. The bridge has since been rebuilt.

Symbols of American departure.

Rice farmers unload rice seedlings from a cart, then transplant them into the flooded paddies. In the distance farmers scoop water from one field to another.

Azolla pinata cultivated in Nghe An province as green manure. Only recently, U.
agronomists have belatedly discovered that azolla in symbiosis with blue-green algae mak
nitrogen available in large quantities to crops.

Mechanized soy bean farming on the September Second State Farm, Hoa Bir
province. September 2, 1945 was the day the Democratic Republic of Vietnam w
established.

Workers in June 1973 restore the lines in the southern town of Dong Ha, now administered by the Provisional Revolutionary Government.

Bai Thuong Dam in Thanh Hoa province (DRV), being repaired after damage caused by U.S. bombs, 1973.

Improving hog production at Dien Bien Phu State Farm, site of historic 1954 defeat of the French. Tran Cong Thuy, pictured here, was a member of a Viet Minh assault squad. Later, in 1966, he was able to train the farm's hogs to head for bomb shelters whenever U.S. aircraft attacked.

Liberation Army fighter tells combat stories to children in the PRG area of South Vietnam, 1973.

Soldiers being entertained on the 29th anniversary of the founding of the Vietnam People's Army, 1973.

Vietnam's future. (photo by Ann Dockery, LNS).

Water, Rice and Men

Hung Yen Province, November 1963—

The Old and the New

The season of the heavy skies has passed. There can still be a downpour, but not the heavy rain or summer typhoon that can bring to a standstill life in a whole region. On a sunny day, under an almost Mediterranean blue sky, a light breeze announcing the cold of the winter ripples the yellow ears of the ripening rice. Harvest time has not yet come, so the peasants can spare some time to talk with you or welcome you in for the night. This is not the first time journalists have come here. The previous harvest, the most important one, has already been weighed, the balance sheet drawn up, and next year's plan drafted. It is an ideal time to go by bicycle, the most practical means of transportation here, into the countryside. The villages are still situated off the main roads, hidden behind thick bamboo hedges, a sign of the past when the peasant was wary of all who came by road—colonial officials, foreign legionnaires, customs inspectors, mandarins.

You can ride for miles and miles through Hung Yen province on village by-roads without going over a single hill and without seeing a single stone or a single pebble except those brought from afar by man for some building purpose. This is the Red River delta region. Hung Yen province stretches for over 25 miles as the crow flies—44 if meanders are taken into account—on the left bank of the river, born of nothing but age-old silt deposits and embedded in the angle made by the main stream and its tributary, the Luoc River. Along the roads there is rice, of course, as far as the eye can see. The provincial capital has a population of more than 8,000, while the largest rural villages have as many as 6,000 people. The capital is really only a small town. It looks like any other village, only larger, except for its few administrative buildings and its small, pretty, crescent-shaped pond surrounded by newly-planted coconut trees. This is because the only activity in the province is agriculture.

This is the heart of the Red River delta, where population growth and density are among the highest in the world. Below are some figures on the population and the average per capita area of arable land (the province is less than 347

This essay was first published in Vietnamese Studies, *No. 2 (Hanoi: 1964); and was reprinted in* La Pensée, *No. 122, August 1965;* Tradition et Révolution au Vietnam, *Chesneaux, Boudarel and Hemery, eds. (Paris: Editions Anthropos, 1971); and* Expériences Vietnamiennes, *Nguyen Khac Vien (Paris: Editions Sociales, 1971). Hung Yen has now been incorporated into Hai Hung province.*

square miles in size and has about 170,000 acres of arable land):

Population and Per Capita Arable Land in Hung Yen

	1928	*1957*	*1960*	*1962*
Population	392,396	459,910	609,341	646,734
Land per person (sq. yds.)	——	1,798	1,464	1,378
Density per square mile	1,142	——	——	1,890

Hung Yen is thus typical of provinces in the Red River delta. It is overpopulated, exclusively agricultural, and its problem of hunger has remained unsolved for centuries. We have therefore chosen this province for our inquiry, hoping to find answers to some urgent questions. Has Hung Yen been able to overcome famine these last few years under the new regime? Has it found a means of developing its agriculture? Have people had to resign themselves to a state of permanent food scarcity and to a catastrophic famine each time a disaster occurs, or have they found a way to conquer nature?

All these questions were on my mind as we rode from village to village on our bikes, passing fragrant rice fields and creaking bamboo hedges. Along the small dikes, little buffalo boys were taking their animals to pasture, while in the courtyards the early rice was being threshed by hand. Here and there, in the mud-walled cottages, one could hear the muffled thud of rice pestles worked by diligent feet. Along the way, we came across people carrying shoulder poles at both ends balancing baskets of rice, fruit, bricks and manure. When we stopped at an inn under the shade of a banyan tree, an old woman with lacquered teeth, chewing betel, served us rice cakes and a bowl of steaming tea. The past was certainly with us. Had we been able to go back to the sixteenth or seventeenth century, to the time of the Le kings or the Trinh lords, we would have seen the same shoulder poles, rice pestles, buffalo boys, and the same old woman with her thatch-roofed, mud-walled hut. I was momentarily seized with apprehension at the thought that the country might never be able to free itself from its age-old backwardness and feed its rapidly rising population.

On the other hand, we could see indications that the province was undergoing many profound changes. Immediately apparent were electric pumping stations supplied by a high tension power line of 35 kilovolts, helping to bring water easily and quietly to the rice fields separated by small dikes, on land where rice was still being threshed by hand. Yet not all that is new is necessarily "modern." Visitors might unsuspectingly bypass many innovations. If you came upon an ox-cart laden with bricks, you might assume that it came from an age-old past; but in fact the ox-cart dates back barely ten years. Traditionally people carried loads on their backs, and the rubber tires and ball-bearings of the ox-cart show that it is one of those recently "improved" tools. If you saw a village path that was wide and straight and bordered with trees, you could bet a thousand to one that it was built only a few years ago. Most of the trees here are long an trees, quite young yet producing a delicious fruit at an early age. They are carefully surrounded by earth banks planted with cacti whose spine clusters protect them from the buffalo. Look inside the earth bank and you will see a small vegetable garden. The people who planted the trees have carried out the principle that the earth must yield something before the long an trees bear fruit. We once inquisitively looked into the basket hanging from a young peasant's shoulder pole. On top of the unhusked rice we saw a book. The shoulder pole dates back a thousand years, but a simple peasant reading in his leisure time is quite new.

We mentioned the village by-roads, wide and straight, without useless curves. But what is even more striking in Hung Yen province are the irrigation canals, as straight as the streets of New York. A meandering canal almost always indicates that it is an old tributary of the river, or that it was dug long ago, while a canal that runs perfectly straight for many miles must be only a few years old. Here a straight line is a sign of the new, a meander a vestige of the old. Roads and canals in the old days, (that is, up to 1955) went around every mound of earth and followed the divisions of private property. The new men of Hung Yen cut straight lines, no longer hindered by private ownership.

Traces of a more recent past, a sinister past, are still there along the roads: blockhouses of the French Expeditionary Corps, concrete monsters, scattered over the delicately outlined plain, with a gun sometimes absurdly pointing toward the sky. These are the only remaining vestiges of colonialism.

Thinking about this mixture of the old and the new, we tried to get a clearer view of what happened here. We tried to find out how Hung Yen charted its course of development, and whether it has succeeded.

Doctrine and Practical Experience

In his spare time, the secretary of the Party Committee of Hung Yen province accompanied us and gave us his comments:

"When peace was reestablished at the end of 1954 and we came back from the *maquis* to take charge of administration of Hung Yen, the only things we inherited from the former regime for a province of half a million souls were a jeep, a bike, and an entirely destroyed provincial capital. This was all we had for our administration. Two hundred villages had been ravaged, 70 of them razed. We had only 3,800 buffalo to work 170,000 acres of land. The French Expeditionary Corps in fact had special instructions to massacre all buffalo to prevent the farming of the land. Hunger was the occupiers' best ally. In many villages, men harnessed themselves to their plows. The dikes had not been repaired or adequately maintained since 1939. One hundred thousand people were on the verge of starvation during the dry spell at the end of 1954 and the beginning of 1955. Nine years of occupation by colonial troops had left these effects: ten thousand people afflicted with venereal disease and 20,000 people, mostly peasants, press-ganged into the puppet army. We recovered 7,000 tons of barbed wire from fences around military posts and 10,000 steel helmets which the peasants have used for cooking pots.

"What was to be done? Our government provided relief to ward off the famine of that year, but we could not go on living on subsidies indefinitely, the more so as we had struggled during the resistance under the slogan of relying essentially on ourselves. Hung Yen, an agricultural province, not only did not receive relief food, but on the contrary was expected to supply foodstuffs and other agricultural products to the government.

"As Marxists, we have a doctrine that calls for abolishing the old feudal production relations through radical land reform, setting up agricultural cooperatives to encourage the development of productive forces, and within this new framework increasing the use of technical improvements and encouraging production to raise the peasants' standard of living and contribute to the building of socialism in the country as a whole. In the desolation of the post-war ruins, which evoked the ocean of sufferings described in Buddhist scriptures, we were not without a compass. With each step forward, resolutions and directives from the [Party] Central Committee provided us with precise instructions on how to proceed to the next stage.

"To use a compass to find one's way in the woods is one thing, but to blaze a path through a maze of agricultural problems is something else. We could rely on the age-old experience of the peasants, however. Compass in hand, we thus groped our way forward, since none of the province leaders was an agronomist or water conservation expert. Our average level of instruction was barely above primary school. Our only principle of action was to stay close to the peasant masses, and to follow faithfully the directions given by the

Central Committee. Now, after nine years of trials and experiments, we think we have found both a theoretical and practical doctrine.

"But take a look at the facts and figures yourselves."

As in all the other provinces, land reform was thoroughly carried out from 1954 to 1956. As elsewhere, errors were committed, but they were quickly corrected in 1957. The reforms made it possible to ascertain the different categories of the peasantry.

Social Categories in Hung Yen

	Number of Households	Number of People	Percent of Population
Landlords	3,535	17,013	2.9
Rich peasants	1,913	11,904	2.0
Middle peasants	44,846	208,775	35.7
Poor and landless peasants	88,829	346,911	59.4
Total	139,123	584,603	100.0

Land reform, by allocating land to more than half the peasantry, rapidly stimulated production within the framework of individual ownership, and as early as 1956 the pre-war level of production was surpassed. It was also possible to mobilize the peasants for repairing dikes and dredging old canals. Even by 1957, 171,600 tons[1] of unhusked rice were produced, outstripping the 145,000 tons reached in 1939, the best year before the war.

Nevertheless, even though famine was avoided, production was still hindered by natural disasters and the tiny size of individual plots—most of them an acre or smaller—preventing any prospect of technical improvements or investment. Vietnamese leaders, as dedicated Marxists, launched the

[1] Short tons.—*Ed.*

agricultural cooperatives campaign in 1958, only a year after land reform was completed, and Hung Yen was among the first to form cooperatives. As a matter of fact, during the liberation war the peasants had already begun to form mutual aid teams which by 1957 included nearly 74 percent of the population. At the beginning of 1958, three cooperatives were established in various regions of the province. In the winter of 1958-59, on the basis of this first experiment, 222 new cooperatives were formed, comprising 39.2 percent of the population. Then, in the middle of 1959, a course on cooperatives was given in many localities and was attended by 25,000 Party members, village cadres, and members of popular organizations. One thousand two hundred and seven cooperatives were set up, encompassing 54 percent of the population in two waves during 1959. Throughout 1960 the campaign kept expanding, and by the end of the year 108,740 households, or 93 percent of the population, had joined cooperatives, the total number of which reached 1,408.

During this period, 332 cooperatives included more than 100 households each, four had more than 300 households, and the average cooperative numbered between 50 and 80 households cultivating 65 to 90 acres. By 1961 practically all the peasants of Hung Yen had joined cooperatives, and individual cultivation had completely disappeared.

But, as President Ho Chi Minh said, one does not form an association just for fun. Output had to be increased, famine eliminated once and for all, floods and drought combated, and quality and volume of production improved. Structural problems, such as carrying out land reform and cooperativization, were emphasized until 1960, but increasing output became the central problem as soon as coooperativization was completed. The new forms of production could not be set up by the will of the leaders and Party militants alone. The cooperatives had to be built on new material bases and new production techniques. The Third National Congress of the Workers' Party, held in September

1960, and the July 1961 Resolution on Agricultural Development, adopted at the Fifth Plenary Session of the Party Central Committee, charted the course for agricultural development for the leaders of Hung Yen. Simultaneous with the start of the cooperativization campaign in 1958, another battle was launched which would give Hung Yen the material foundation for its new agricultural structure.

The Battle to Tame the Water

On January 5, 1958, in the main square of the provincial capital President Ho Chi Minh spoke to a crowd of tens of thousands of people who had come from all over the province. The people were greatly moved by their first glimpse of the leader they had been talking about for 30 years, whose name had been linked with every episode of Vietnamese contemporary history. Ho Chi Minh called on them to launch a new battle, not against cruel and greedy men this time, but against hostile nature. Then he walked throughout the province to work out the plan of operation. The trail was blazed and from then on, the main target was to tame the waters, a goal which became a real obsession for the leaders and people of Hung Yen. Plans were carried out, and in every household people got ready to answer the President's call. "Water conservation fever" spread throughout the province. Everybody talked about canals, sluice gates, embankments, earth digging, volume of water transported, level reached. The roads were crowded with people en route to construction sites, each with his or her own supply of rice and food and even firewood for cooking. Many walked as far as 15 or 25 miles from their own villages or hamlets.

People knew from their own experience how precious water is, but also how dangerous it could be. Until then they had barely managed to protect themselves—quite inadequately—against the treacherous waters. During the rainy season, from May to October, as much as a foot of rain could fall in one day. When the Red River swells its level reaches 30 or even 40 feet, and the dikes have to be raised. The banks of the river and its tributary, the Luoc, are lined with about 85 miles of dikes which are almost ten centuries old. Under the old dynasties and the colonial regime, the dikes might protect the province against average flood crests, but in a bad year the waters would break through the dikes in fury, submerging many score acres of land, washing away houses, drowning cattle, and ruining crops.

Thus the dikes prevented floods from occurring every year and permitted the population to survive. Yet, under this system existence would always be poor, because while providing protection, the dikes also took away the most precious commodity to a rice-growing region: water. Although it rains heavily in Hung Yen, as in the Red River delta as a whole, the province's yearly 72 inches of rain fall exclusively from May to October. During the rest of the year, spells of drought can last as long as several months, making cultivation impossible. The rich, silt-laden waters of the Red River roll majestically between the dikes, while the powerless peasants look helplessly at their scorched rice fields.

For centuries, when a dry spell had dragged on for months, the peasants would gather in long processions, burn votive offerings, sacrifice pigs and recite prayers in honor of the gods, their efforts profiting only a few priests. This was going on in some places until 1951, the secretary of the Party Committee told us. Then, too, when it had rained heavily, water accumulated in low-lying regions, submerging immense areas of rice fields and ruining the rice, because the dikes prevented the water from draining away.

"As you ride through the province, you may think that the land is all flat," said the Party secretary, "but the water levels show that there are gradations." From the water standpoint, Hung Yen is divided into four regions: the northwest, a high-lying region ten to 25 feet above sea level; the low-lying southeast, from two to six-and-a-half feet above sea level; in between, a middle region from six-and-a-half to ten feet above sea level. On the other side of the dikes is the fourth region—stretches of land which can be cultivated during the dry season but which are submerged when the river is high.

The "highlands" can be cultivated only in the rainy season and the "lowlands" during the dry season; the "midlands" yield two crops a year, since they can keep out enough water during the dry season and drain the surplus when the rains come. But the whims of nature sometimes belie these calculations. A dry spell lasts 15 days longer than usual, and a whole crop is lost. A typhoon or storm comes, and it becomes impossible to drain the water out of large areas. "Either the rice rots or it's scorched," went a popular saying that expressed the hard life of people trying to wrest a meager living from this harsh land.

From the records of the Nguyen dynasty, we learn that in the course of the nineteenth century, the crop was lost 44 times. The dikes of the Red River burst 16 times in the last quarter of the nineteenth century, turning the whole of Khoai Chau district into a swamp soon taken over by reeds. In a report written in 1901, a French colonial official named Miribel complained that a river as large as the Red River could still cross the province without supplying it with a single drop of water.[2] Thirty years later, in 1932, the mandarin who governed as province chief wrote in a report to the colonial authorities:

"The Hung Yen farmers are clamoring for water." Then he dreamed about the future:

> When the rice fields bring in two harvests a year, Hung Yen, a purely agricultural province, will be one of the best granaries in Tonkin. The number of wrongdoers will decline, public welfare

[2] Details on Hung Yen during the colonial period are taken from two reports, one written in 1901 by the French administrator Miribel and the second in 1932 by the mandarin province chief. They are kept in the Hanoi Central Library (numbers M.10,357 and 10,358). We will refer to them here as the Miribel Report and the Mandarin Report.

services will increase in number, and economic prosperity will lead to full administrative stability.

Colonial officials and mandarins of long ago may have contented themselves by writing laments or pious wishes, but it was up to the new regime to find a way to quench the age-old thirst of Hung Yen.

As early as 1958, with its war damage barely repaired, the Democratic Republic of Vietnam started to grapple with the Red River. An opening was cut through the dike at Xuan Quan and fitted with powerful concrete sluices. The river water, brought in via a big canal, irrigated the rice fields of three provinces, including Hung Yen. It was called the Bac Hung Hai Irrigation Network. But this big canal and other works would not have been of much use if the population had not dug thousands of small canals and supply and storage arteries, allowing the silt-laden water to flow throughout the province. Within the locality or area managed by each cooperative, the slightest difference in ground level meant an excess of water in one place or a scarcity in another. A system was thus needed to create large areas of more or less the same level, within which water could be stored by means of small dikes. For several years, from 1958 to 1963, it was a story of millions: the central and provincial administrations spent millions of *dong;*[3] millions of workdays were provided by the population, and millions of cubic yards of earth were moved.

As a result we now have more than 2,400 miles of canals of all sizes which, together with ten electric pumping stations, ensure the irrigation of 136,750 acres. The works to be undertaken in 1964 will make it possible to irrigate the rest of the land and drain 20,000 acres. At present—the end of 1963—Hung Yen can boast that it no longer suffers from drought. In the winter of 1962-63, after it had not rained for

---

[3] Vietnamese unit of currency, with an official exchange rate of about five to the U.S. dollar.—*Ed.*

Table of "the Millions"

	Earth Moved (cu. yds.)	Workdays Workdays	State Expenditures (dong)
1958	2,350,000	1,200,000	1,240,000
1959	5,100,000	3,320,000	1,580,000
1960	12,000,000	6,320,000	1,640,000
1961	13,100,000	8,310,000	3,374,000
1962	16,600,000	9,810,000	4,067,000
1963 (9 months)	10,200,000	— —	4,380,000

months, Hung Yen was nevertheless able to plant its summer rice seedlings ahead of schedule (at the end of January). The draining of low-lying areas during heavy rainfall is still inadequate; however, in August and September of 1963, by mobilizing thousands of people, we succeeded in draining the flooded rice fields into the canals leading to the Luoc River.

A Peaceful Dien Bien Phu [4]

This is what happened on January 6, 1961 in An Vu village, two miles from the district center:

At noon the "Rocket" units (youth units) were brought by trucks to the planned positions. An Vu village was as noisy as on a festival day, with banners everywhere. Members of the Rocket units were wearing armbands bearing the inscription, "We Are Determined to Win." Units from My Hao and Tien Lu had flags on the handles of their hoes and spades given to them at the Bac Hung Hai construction site. They proudly marched behind their Party Committees' banners, on which were embroidered the slogan, "The Best Water Conservation Work." Everyone was

[4]Dien Bien Phu, a valley in North Vietnam near the Laotian border, was the location of the strategic battle won by the Vietnam People's Army in May 1954, signaling the collapse of the French empire in Indochina.—*Ed.*

determined to win the construction site's Flag of Honor for his unit.

Thousands of people were streaming to their reserved positions. Here and there songs had started and groups were singing back and forth to each other. A group of young girls was singing out challenges to the boys, and the white beards of the old mixed with young faces.

Right after the inauguration ceremony, each unit returned to its assigned place, the flags were set up in bright red rows in the fields, and thousands of people spread out to work.

Difficulties occurred the first day. A bitterly cold wind blew in. Many Rocket units had to work in flooded areas for long hours, sometimes standing waist-high in the muddy water. Though shivering with cold, they kept on singing and shouting slogans. Several units asked to be allowed to work all night to complete their tasks. All wanted to break the records previously set by other Rocket units.

The first evening, each village called together its Party militants and youth members, who had promised to achieve higher standards and carry out their assigned tasks ahead of schedule. Many had bought new tools out of their own pockets to speed up their work. Experiences were shared during visits. Slogans on the flags said, "Don't let tools lie idle!" and, "Forward, for our brothers in the South!"

Every day, province and district leaders came to supervise the work and encourage the workers, and cadres were sent to the villages to mobilize other workers. The achievements of elite units or individual workers were broadcast several times a day over the loudspeaker network. In the evening or during breaks there were performances by well-known artists or amateur singers chosen from among the workers at the construction site.

Both comrade Ha Huy Giap, a member of the Central Committee, and the vice minister of water conservation came from the capital to talk to the workers. Leaders, cadres and officials in the provincial administration and army units came to work beside the peasants in the mud. State employees in the Supply Services moved an average of 729 cubic feet of earth per day. Old Mr. Ton gathered a group of 15 old people around him, some of them over 68 years old.

The "rear" also participated actively. Women and the

elderly, sometimes from faraway villages, came and gave gifts to the workers. Children from neighboring schools came to pay visits to their "aunts and uncles" on the work site. The workers were able to stay in the homes of the local people and helped them with their chores.[5]

Thus, in 15 days, a canal 8,860 feet long, 66 feet wide and ten feet deep, paralleled by a road 40 feet wide, had been completed by over 5,000 workers coming from all the villages in the province. In the course of this work, 389 workers received honorary diplomas, five were admitted to the Party and 83 to youth organizations. In the years that followed, the remaining part of the Dien Bien Phu Canal was completed in the same atmosphere and rhythm. This 17-mile-long canal crosses the entire width of the province and is the main food artery as well as the best transport waterway in Hung Yen. Many smaller arteries fan out from this main canal, bringing water—life itself— to tens of thousands of acres of land.

Other great canals have also been dug—the Peace Canal and the Ho Chi Minh Canal—which became the sources of thousands of smaller ones. The map of Hung Yen now looks like a leaf with an intricate network of veins. Red River water now penetrates into the heart of each village, not by rushing through a burst dike, but led by the hand of man, from sluice to sluice, from canal to canal. Do Hung Yen people not have every reason to baptize their greatest achievement in water conservation with the prestigious name of victory, "Dien Bien Phu"?

While canals were being dug along one side of the dikes, on the other side embankments were built on land that had been periodically submerged by high waters. A second dike was built alongside the first, following the river and fitted with sluices to allow the water to flow in and out. A young girl named Phan Thi Vach suggested that the island of Hung

[5] From the report sent by the construction site leadership for the first part of the Dien Bien Phu Canal.

Cuong in the middle of the Red River be surrounded by dikes and turned into a mosaic of little plots to grow crops even during the rainy season. Her suggestion was carried out and she was awarded the most honored title in the Democratic Republic of Vietnam, that of Labor Hero.

From One Campaign to Another

Hung Yen peasants used to rely essentially on the one main rice crop per year—harvested in May in the lowlands and in November in the highlands. When the rainfall was favorable, a second harvest was possible. Thus, even though the amount of available arable land did not vary much, the surface actually cultivated did fluctuate considerably from year to year. Everything depended on the whims of nature. By using its water reserves wisely and making great efforts, Hung Yen succeeded in growing an average of 50,000 acres of rice for the May harvest and 125,000 for the November one. Now, however, almost all the land yields two harvests per year. The amount of arable land has decreased annually because of construction and the growing population, but the cultivated area has increased because of better irrigation. Of course, rainfall always affects the extension of crops or increase of yields (1959, for instance, was an exceptionally favorable year), but despite considerable yearly variations there has been a regular increase in cultivated area and yields.

Cultivated Area and Production in Hung Yen

	1958	*1959*	*1960*	*1961*	*1962*
Arable acres	168,233	165,389	166,657	169,893	169,893
Acres cultivated[6]	242,667	281,098	277,253	304,963	295,257
Tons of rice	182,213	233,654	172,569	207,962	202,798

[6]May and November crops combined.—*Ed.*

While Hung Yen's population increased from 549,000 in 1957 to more than 640,000 in 1962, the per capita area of land under cultivation and food production (rice and other food crops calculated according to their rice equivalents) increased respectively from .481 to .509 acre, and from 752.4 to 849.2 pounds. Agricultural growth has thus out-stripped demographic growth—a remarkable feat for an underdeveloped country—in a region in which population density is practically 1,200 per square mile.

Since 1961, an autumn rice crop has been harvested in between the usual two, in July and August, on about 10,000 acres. Thus, good irrigation and the adoption of fast-growing varieties of rice (the Nam Ninh strain in particular) enable some of the land to yield as many as three crops a year now.

If you scan the statistics on Hung Yen, you will come across the interesting fact that the area planted with jute, an industrial crop, and various tubers has increased each year. The monoculture of rice is giving way to polyculture, to a more diversified agriculture. It is only a beginning, but when one takes a walk on the smaller roads of Hung Yen, the changes are already visible. Fields planted with jute, with their slender stems, red leaves and white flowers, make vivid splashes among the vast rice fields. The Hung Yen country-side no longer resembles the traditional picture of the Vietnamese countryside. The growth in jute cultivation, by area, is as follows:

Jute Cultivation in Hung Yen (in acres)

1957	1958	1959	1960	1961	1962
2,206	2,188	2,941	6,763	5,952	9,232

The poor peasant of Hung Yen used to be satisifed if he could merely subsist after the rice harvest; he asked for no more. Landlords sold the rice they had extorted, grain by grain, from their tenants. Sixteen thousand eight hundred tons of rice were exported from the province every year. While the people did not have enough to live on, they allowed the landlords to "make enough money" to buy luxury products like silk clothes, carved wood furniture, and even luxury goods from Paris. Nowadays, however, everyone is assured of enough to eat, and the cooperatives make their money by increasing jute production and selling it to the state.

Nevertheless, multiple crop growing decreases the nutrients in the soil more rapidly, so the fertilizer problem has become acute. Green compost, chemical fertilizers bought from the state, and quicklime for acid soils all have been used to enrich the soil. The silt brought in by the Red River water has proved very beneficial. But until the chemical era arrives in Hung Yen, manure will remain the principal source of fertilizer. Pig manure is the leading fertilizer because the extensive pasture land required to raise buffalo and oxen cannot be found in this overpopulated province where every inch of land must be used to best advantage. Finding food for the pigs is a problem, however, since the land can barely meet the needs of its human population. The usual pig feed is a mixture of rice bran, finely cut banana trunks, and a few aquatic plants. If the number of pigs were increased, there would not be enough bran to feed them. The land thus must yield enough to feed both men and pigs, and the monoculture of rice cannot solve this problem. Crops must be found that give much more starch than rice, whose yield, despite better irrigation methods, is still only around .9 ton per acre (compared to .6 ton in 1939) because of limited supplies of fertilizer. The cultivation of various tubers, which yield at least ten times as much starch, can alone solve the problem of producing more food for a growing population and for the pigs, which supply meat as well as manure.

Peasants traditionally grew sweet potatoes on dry land. In times of food scarcity and in pre-harvest periods, the sweet potato was the "rice" of the poor. But after land reform, sweet potato cultivation somewhat decreased. The poor peasant has enough rice now, so he turns his back on the sweet potato, which recalls the misery of the past. Sweet potato production in Hung Yen dropped from 22,400 tons in 1957 to less than 14,600 tons in 1962. But urban growth caused by industrialization presented urgent supply problems, and increasing pig production became a crucial need. It would be interesting to compare the present situation in Vietnam on the eve of industrialization with that prevailing in Europe toward the end of the eighteenth century, when large-scale industry began to appear. The rise in potato production enabled European countries to get enough food for their growing cities at a time when the wheat yield stayed the same as it had been for centuries.

Vietnam has an advantage over eighteenth century Europe, though. Sweet potatoes and other tubers, either aquatic or grown on dry land, are already familiar to the peasants. Recultivating the sweet potato and developing the other tubers (*Colocasia antiquorum, Marunta arundinacea*) is thus a relatively easy task. Hung Yen has set an example: the areas set aside for the aquatic taro (*Colocasia*) and *Marunta arundinacea* have been increased. (Nineteen hundred sixty was an insignificant year.)

Tuber Production in Hung Yen

| | 1961 | | 1962 | | 1963 |
	Acres	Tons	Acres	Tons	Acres
Aquatic taro	1,597	16,170	1,950	21,450	6,000
Marunta arundinacea	3,125	24,780	3,250	27,880	4,325

The pig herds have likewise increased from 102,860 in 1957 to 156,470 in 1962.

Fish breeding in rice fields and ponds has brought in a supplementary income to the peasants and has supplied a new source of protein to their diet. Thirty thousand acres of water are now used for this purpose, and the area keeps increasing. Agricultural cooperatives are building brick-kilns, lime-kilns, wood-working shops and forges; they have started raising silkworms, too. All these secondary trades bring in appreciable returns. Since 1960, a widespread movement has been launched to decongest the overpopulated plains of the delta. In the last three years, 12,000 people have left the plains for the mountain regions, where they have already settled 10,000 acres of land.

"We're working non-stop," said the Party secretary. "After the water conservation problem, we had the fertilizer problem, then the matter of seeds, then land settlement in the mountains, then the problem of the fruit trees, fast-growing strains of rice, fish breeding, jute, lime-kilns. I could go on for days enumerating the problems Hung Yen has had to deal with. One campaign hardly comes to an end before another one begins."

But the Hung Yen leaders show no signs of weariness, as though they take pleasure in seeking out new problems that need to be resolved. Formerly, bee keeping and sticklac[7] production were unknown in the province. Then one of the Hung Yen leaders happened to stay for some time in the mountain region and on his return set up some experimental stations for bees and sticklac. As we walked across the countryside with the leaders, they pointed out not only the rice and jute fields but the orchards of long an, orange and mandarin trees, carefully grafted and lovingly tended by expert hands. "All these fruit trees bring us foreign exchange," said the president of the province Administrative Committee, his eyes flashing with pride. For the people of Hung Yen, more foreign exchange means more electric pumps, tractors, chemical fertilizers, and more transistor radios to put them in touch with the rest of the world.

Hung Yen is still an agricultural province, but its

---

[7]Sticklac is the secretion of female scale insects which is used to produce shellac and red dye.—*Ed.*

resources are increasing and becoming more diversified, an undeniable sign of significant progress. For peasants in the underdeveloped countries, progress consists not only in having more rice or sweet potatoes, but also in having more varied food and "making money" from more and more diversified sources. It is interesting in this regard to look at the distribution of agricultural income in the province from 1957 to 1962, in millions of *dong*:

Income from Agriculture in Hung Yen

	Food Crops	Industrial Crops	Animal Breeding	Fish Raising	Other	Non-food Crop Total
1957	37.6	2.3	7.6	0	12.6	22.50 (37%)
1962	46.0	4.6	14.0	1.8	15.9	36.31 (44%)

From the Family Plot to Collective Effort

Digging canals, planting jute or tubers, breeding fish or introducing a new rice strain—are these all questions of applied agronomy? These techniques are brought into play at the cooperative level, so instead of engaging in an academic discussion of the problem, let us visit some of these coops, look at their history and analyze their activities.

An Vi Coop in Khoai Chau district is in the upper part of the province, which was once notorious for its beggars. Half the land in An Vi village was owned by eight landlords. Driven out by hunger, many poor peasants had to leave their homes to find work on rubber plantations in the South or in the mines of faraway New Caledonia. One of them, Cu Thuong, came home recently from the New Hebrides, at the age of 82. Others found the only way out of their desperate situation was conversion to Catholicism, which at least gave them the hope of a better life after death. It also gave the colonialists and the reactionaries a relatively solid hold on the village. The resistance and land reform, however, opened the eyes of many Catholics.

In 1959, fifty households participated in discussions to decide whether they should follow capitalism or socialism and to talk about the problems of cooperativization. Rumors immediately began to circulate that God would abandon you if you joined the coop. You would have to work all the time without stopping. You would have to ask the permission of the management committee to celebrate any family ceremonies. Your work would benefit only the cadres. Look at the birds, said the rumors: they do not have to get together in groups to be productive; God sees to it that each one is guaranteed its livelihood. Out of the 45 households that had applied for membership, 12, shaken by these rumors, withdrew. There were Catholics, however, among the 33 that remained in the coop. Most of the land yielded only one rice crop, harvested in November, and several secondary food crops such as sweet potatoes, corn and beans. It was rough going at first, but in the course of 1960, after the state-built irrigation network was completed, the coop succeeded in digging on its own land a series of canals totaling nearly 10,000 feet. The volume of earth moved during the year reached 105 cubic feet per person. As an immediate result, the area devoted to May rice and secondary food crops—that is to say, all crops grown during the dry season—rapidly increased. This success encouraged other households to join, and in 1961 the coop membership reached the present level of 215 households (989 people), among them 157 Catholic households. The number of adults with full working capacity was 372, with women making up almost two-thirds of the total number.

The coop worked 206.5 *mau*[8] with 12 buffalo, 25 oxen, 38 plows, 38 harrows, and total liquid assets amounting to 25,375 *dong*. The most important result was the increase in the area planted with summer rice: eleven *mau* in 1960, 54 in 1961, 67 in 1962. Secondary food crops were grown on 71 *mau* in 1960, 107.8 *mau* in 1962. Jute occupied

[8]One *mau* is just under an acre.—*Ed.*

17.2 *mau* in 1960 and 36 in 1962. Each member put in 87 workdays for the coop in 1960, 97 in 1961 and 116 in 1962. Does this mean that everything was going well in An Vi? Far from it.

At the beginning of 1963, like other coops all over the country, An Vi engaged in a campaign for the "improvement of management" with the help of cadres sent by the provincial administration. The purpose was to submit the activities of the past three years to a critical examination, first by Party militants and cadres, then by the whole coop membership, to bring about a noticeable improvement in management. For several days, militants and cadres carefully studied the Resolution on Agricultural Development adopted at the Fifth Plenum of the Central Committee, to adapt its principles to local conditions. Then, the youth, the women and the old people formed small discussion groups. The management committee and the Party cell were responsible for drawing up a detailed balance sheet of the past three years. "We had to start from the beginning," said the coop manager, "five times in a row, but we were encouraged by higher cadres who recommended that we take as much time as necessary." Everyone felt that "something was going to happen," though opinion varied on what would come out of this campaign for improved management.

People had different opinions. Some shrugged their shoulders, saying that the same thing would happen as before, when technical standards were established— meaning that nothing would come of it. A few cadres were worried, thinking that they would have to give up their places to the young. Those members who had served in the puppet administration or army during the war asked themselves whether they would be "purged" or not. A few who did not agree with the cadres rubbed their hands and proclaimed they would "get even" with them. But during the preparatory meetings the cadres quickly oriented the discussions toward problems of production and management. What was going wrong with the coop? Had anyone found a good way to increase production? Had good work discipline been achieved? Were relations with the state good? People had to be encouraged to give their opinions freely, so that short-comings and errors could be uncovered. The wives of a few cadres were taken aside and assured that if their husbands had to sustain any criticism in public, this would be a mark of esteem and confidence.

The day of the general meeting approached. After the report was read, the criticism began. It was learned that one Party cadre had done no field work for three years; that some Party cadres had not worked on production problems; that some members of the management committee had been more concerned with their own team than with the interests of the coop as a whole; that piece-work contracts had been drawn up but never carried out, so that people no longer believed in them; that some people did not want to grow jute because harvesting the plant gave them scabies and retting it was just too hard, so they had grown jute on low-lying plots where it should not have been grown because of the high risk of failure; that many members lost a lot of time waiting for each other to go to the fields but lost no time when the gong rang for rest time. Some team members, when they heard the gong, even went so far as to empty the water they had just scooped up back into the irrigation canal. In the work teams, some of the more energetic people often got together to earn the maximum number of workdays and workpoints. Women assigned to transplant seedlings knew that their work had been poorly prepared and would be to no avail, but they had completed their tasks without complainung under these unfavorable conditions because they did not dare criticize the cadres.

The meeting was very animated and in this atmosphere testimonies were given and self-criticism came forth spon-taneously. A 72-year-old woman cried out, "I used to be a wretched concubine living on handouts. Now, thanks to the coop, I have enough rice to eat and even a 150-pound pig that I will sell to the state." A Party militant, after much hesitation, made his self-criticism: "I had a 130-pound pig which people told me to sell to the state, but one night I took it to sell on the free market. No one knew the truth because I told people that the pig had been sold to the state. This happened in 1960."

As for the production plan, many things became clearer to everybody. No adequate study had been made on the possible uses for the various kinds of land and not enough attention had been given to the development of tubers and industrial crops. Obligations toward the state had been neglected, in spite of the fact that it was the state which helped the peasants build the big irrigation works and which supplied them with chemical fertilizers and all kinds of commodities. The number of workdays had increased, but their value had declined year after year because of decreasing yields: 1.47 *dong* in 1960, 1.29 in 1961, 1.14 in 1962. Therefore, it was necessary to develop animal breeding and more profitable industrial crops, particularly jute, the cultivation of which would increase from 41 *mau* in 1963 to 57 *mau* in 1964. Pig breeding would be carried out both on the household and coop levels. More fruit trees and more bamboo for building purposes would be grown. Since the birth rate had reached 4.7 percent yearly, it was decided to promote the campaign for settlement in the mountain regions, which had started the previous year. The results exceeded the leaders' expectations, however. One hundred eighty-five people with their families offered to go, of whom 125 met the requirements. Dikes were built around an eight-*mau* plot of low-lying land for fish breeding. Six thousand six hundred feet of roads were repaired. An eight-*sau*[9] nursery was entrusted to a group of the elderly for growing saplings. Manure sheds were built. It was decided to send three cadres to the secondary school of agriculture to study, one to learn agricultural techniques, another animal breeding and bee keeping, and the third irrigation and

[9]There are ten *sau to a mau—Ed.*

azolla[10] growing.

Everyone in An Vi felt great enthusiasm at the end of 1963, and there were new plans for increased production.

*   *   *   *   *

The Luu Xa Cooperative of 415 households was set up in the fall of 1959 and owns 80 *mau* (about 75 acres) of rice fields stretching along the Dinh Zu Canal. The dense population there has had to live on very little land. In earlier times people hired themselves out as farmhands in other locations or begged along National Highway No. 5, which passes by the village. At first the coop had only 37 households and 27.5 acres of land in 1959. The May 1960 harvest was not very good, and individual peasants had brought in more than the coop members. Some members asked to leave the coop but were finally persuaded to remain. Then came a long drought in the summer of 1960. The coop dug 1,650 feet of small canals on its land to bring water from the Bac Hung Hai network and succeeded in watering its rice fields by using scooping teams working on five different levels, which would have been impossible for individual peasants to do. Then came another success. The management of the coop had faithfully followed an instruction from above recommending the planting of the fast-growing Nam Ninh variety of rice to obtain an extra harvest in autumn, while individual peasants had hesitated to adopt this new technique. The double success obtained from the harvests of autumn and winter, 1960 persuaded 62 more households to ask to be admitted. The years 1961 and 1962 witnessed other improvements, unfortunately offset by some shortcomings and errors. The total length of irrigation canals and ditches had by then reached 4,950 feet, the area planted with autumn rice had increased, and the well-irrigated lands were yielding two harvests a year on a regular basis. But the construction of a

---

[10]Azolla is a green plant grown in ponds for use as a fertilizer.—*Ed.*

brick-kiln brought about a loss of 260 *dong*, and, following the example of a neighboring village, the coop started planting potatoes and gave up the sweet potato with which it had been more familiar. The potatoes were damaged by the cold, and the harvest was short.

In May 1963, the provincial administration sent a cadre to Luu Xa to launch the campaign for improved management. The cadre, a native of the village, knew the land and people of the coop intimately. He stayed several months to help the management committee, since the coop was considered quite poorly managed. The Party leaders and militants carried out a long period of preparation in order to ascertain the coop's shortcomings and good points. Until then, the management committee had evidently dumped all its responsibilities on the four production teams, reserving for itself the simple role of arbiter. From the management's point of view, each team had become a cooperative in its own right. The person in charge of coop finance tended to confuse the budget of the coop with that of the village administrative committee and, as a result, handed out money for all kinds of public expenditures, such as meetings of young people, the elderly, funerals, and so on. Neither the coop's financial obligations to the state (3,000 *dong*) nor the debts it owed its members (2,000 *dong*) had been paid. Except for the irrigation works, no construction had been undertaken by the coop during the previous three years. The management had several achievements to its credit, however. It had bought six new buffalo and had regularly fulfilled its obligations in unhusked rice and other agricultural products to the state. And it had implemented new techniques like azolla growing and seed preparation.

In the summer of 1963 the cultivation of autumn rice increased and brought in 330-440 pounds of unhusked rice for every household. This success created a new atmosphere. Encouraged, coop members worked even harder to prepare for the year-end harvest. They plowed and harrowed the fields twice and, to compensate for lack of fertilizer, dredged the canals and spread mud on the fields. Some people hesitated over spreading mud, but the management committee decided to give good pay for the work and urged the Party and youth members to set the example. In just a few days, all the fields were covered with a layer of mud drawn from the canals and ponds. It was the same for the weeding. Adequate pay, figured according to the quantity and quality of the work and no longer on an equal basis, put an end to bad work habits.

The campaign for improved management officially started September 2, National Independence Day.[11] It began with festivities, such as processions, musical performances, sports competitions, chess games, and singing. Study sessions and discussions followed, on the basis of the report prepared by the management committee on the previous three years' activities. Production, labor management and finance were each the subject of a discussion. An exhibit of the coop was organized, including a carefully constructed model of the coop's lands, statistical information, graphs on production, reports praising or criticizing individual workers and leaders, information on rice plants and potato tubers from various plots, and data on vegetables and fruits from various gardens and orchards. Well-fed and well-tended buffalo were exhibited next to underfed and neglected ones. Someone thought of borrowing a few things from the state store in a neighboring town to make an exhibit illustrating the relationship between agriculture and industry, but it was decided instead to borrow from the coop members themselves such items as clothing, fabrics, household utensils, bicycles and cement, which the members had originally bought for their own use. The total cost of the exhibit was only nine *dong*.

There was much discussion during the study sessions and in front of the exhibits. Many people visited the exhibits more than once and seemed to be seriously contemplating

---

[11] Commemorating the founding in Hanoi of the Democratic Republic of Vietnam, September 2, 1945.—*Ed.*

their significance. Coop members gave suggestions for the
following year's production plan and analyzed good and bad
examples of workers during the study sessions. Any mis-
givings they may have had about the honesty of the coop
leaders were dispelled by the presentation of a detailed
financial report. They recognized that while the militants and
cadres lacked experience and dynamism they had always
stood firm and tried, despite complaints and sarcastic re-
marks during difficult moments. A new management committee of eight members was elected: four were Party
members and two were members of the youth organization,
and all were under 40 years of age except for one 42-year-old
man. The president was a 23-year-old Party member who had
just completed military service.

Here are a few figures taken from the accounts of the
Luu Xa Coop, which was, to be sure, one of the least
prosperous coops in the country:

Luu Xa Cooperative, 1960-63

	1960	1961	1962	1963
Area cultivated (mau)	55	171	152	— —
Number of pigs	54	160	170	184
Poultry	162	544	484	625
Number of workdays	78	107	106	143
Food production per person (lbs./mo.)	48.4	46.2	48.4	— —
Rcpts. for rice (dong)	10,092	26,685	26,050	— —
Land rent (dong)	4,062	5,245	4,507	— —
Pymt. for workdays (dong)	4,062	9,572	11,307	— —
Tax (dong)	406	— —	1,213	1,337
Accumulated funds (dong)	180	771	1,042	— —

About 60 percent of the coop's income came from its
household section, which includes garden plots, pig and
poultry breeding and certain handicrafts. This is figured in
monetary terms, despite the fact that we do not yet have an

integrated market economy. Although the cooperative sector provided only 40 percent of the coop's cash income, it does assure members of the basic necessities of life. Products supplied by garden plots and handicrafts have a much higher value in money, but what is most important in a country which is just emerging from a subsistence economy is the supply of food. For Luu Xa, where land is extremely scarce, cooperativization has meant that each coop member is assured of 48.5 pounds of food each month. This is the first time this has ever been achieved and is in large part a result of planned rapid crop rotation. But a continuing increase in yield through technological improvements, along with settle-ment of the mountain regions, will be necessary to maintain this result. On the national level, industrialization as well as new techniques of increasing crop yields will eventually provide sufficient resources for such densely populated re-gions as Luu Xa. For now, however, the peasants themselves can already promote agricultural progress by a whole series of agronomic measures which do not require modern scientific methods. But people are needed to make the achievements.

Promoters of Progress

Night comes rapidly to Luu Xa in the month of November. The little kerosene lamp has to be lit by 6 p.m., and still it sheds only a small luminous circle on the table around which we are all seated. We start to go through the accounts and history of the Luu Xa Cooperative with the management committee. A thatch-roofed hut, which has existed for hundreds of years in Vietnam, barefoot peasants dressed in brown, clouds of smoke ascending from their water pipes, the table, the bench, the wooden board which serves as a bed at night—one might say that nothing has changed in this centuries-old setting of peasant life. Outside, a scrawny dog growls at passersby, and bamboo branches squeak in the autumn wind.

As intransigent journalists, we often interrupt our

hosts and ask for precise figures. How many *mau* how many *dong* how many workdays, how much tax? What is the usual amount? What percentage? The chairman relies on his memory, but the more meticulous accountant searches his books. Pages of long columns of figures in school notebooks are brought closer to the light, so that we can take down all the information we need. Statistics. Who can guarantee the accuracy of the figures? Do they really know how to keep accounts? The members of the management committee completed only the first three grades of general education. They have since taken several weeks of supplementary courses on management and accounting, but how can administrators be trained in such a short time?

Yet the facts are there, the books are well kept, and the arithmetic is correct. We checked the addition and multiplication and found no errors. A young man comes in with a notebook in his hand, and we notice that many of these peasants have notebooks with them, some even fountain pens. The young man says to the accountant, in a fairly aggressive manner, "Now, write down the following in your book: A— in my team has planted five trees, so put down this many points for him. Y— has carried such and such amount of manure for the coop, so he is entitled to this many points. . . " The accountant writes down as instructed, but from time to time he stops writing to assert, "Not that. That goes in your team's books and not in the coop's." Life is making our peasants precise and accurate, for only good accounts make good coops.

Someone raises the point that B—, who is taking care of a buffalo, wants a new tether to be bought. But the president says no, because the coop regulations stipulate that small work tools have to be bought by the members themselves and that only important tools such as plows and harrows can be bought with coop money. Since the harvesters buy their own sickles, why can't the buffalo herder buy his own tether?

Other problems come up and are discussed accordingly. One is whether to give thatch to the D— family. Thatch is scarce, winter is coming, and everyone is thinking of adding to his roof. There won't be much this time since it rained several days in a row just when the rice was ripening. There will be many requests for thatch. A clear majority is formed against the D— family. They did not want to give many workdays to the coop. On one occasion, Mr. D— even refused to make bamboo scoops for the coop during the middle of a dry spell. The D—s were more involved in their small-scale itinerant trade than in the coop and, as a result, did not earn very many points during the last harvest. People thought they deserved to go without thatch—it would serve them right. The 23-year-old chairman, lost in thought, lets the discussion go on for a while. Then he gives his opinion: "Yes, the D—s are not cooperative, but their roof is in such a bad state that rain water keeps pouring into their house and their children have to live in constant dampness. As far as thatch is concerned, the most important consideration should be the state of the person's roof rather than the number of work-days or workpoints earned. Let's maintain unity first and foremost. I propose that the D—s be given some thatch. They will get the point in the end, and it will be the best lesson for them."

The D— family got its share of the thatch. As for the lesson, we were the first to understand its significance. Our peasants have become good accountants and very strict on the rules and regulations, tough "businessmen" who haggle to the last point. Their concern is in receiving just reward in their work, not in receiving profit or privilege. Among themselves they are, above all, comrades-in-work. That evening, in this thatch-roofed hut at Luu Xa, lit up by a flickering kerosene lamp, we thought we had found a good definition of socialism: good accounts and good comrade-ship. Just being a good manager was not enough, nor was being a utopian who wants to divide everything into equal parts.

Then we talked about the young people. "What hap-pened at the youth meeting the other day?" we asked the man in charge.

"There were about a hundred of us," he said, "including some young people from other coops, and we met at the former village temple. Lots of girls were there, determined and alert. The secretary of the village's Party cell was there. A visitor who had just returned from France talked to us about French peasants. It seems that over there, peasants who own 25 acres can't make ends meet and demonstrate against their government. In the name of the young people in our coop, we have raised a challenge to see which youth unit will have the best seeds and best experimental plots in the coming year. The girls have challenged us on azolla growing. This year we're going to send one of our people to the provincial secondary school of agriculture to study the latest techniques. We'll have to tighten our belts to pay for his studies."

It was late. We were about to go to bed when someone asked, "What do you think, you journalists, about the *coup d'etat* in the South? What will the Americans do? They must be fed up with Cuba, blacks fighting for their rights, unrest in Venezuela, and U.S. Marines bogged down in the South of our country!" No doubt about it, our peasants are informed about a lot of things that are going on in their world, much better informed, in fact, than the scholars of ancient times. People who still have only 48 pounds of food per month and live in thatch-roofed huts manage to read newspapers and discuss world events. Science, technology, economics, the five-year plan—these are no longer unknown words to them.

That night, I went to bed pondering the significance of this extraordinary fact, that such new men could have appeared in this still quite archaic setting.

From "Bandit" to Guerrilla Fighter

During the political upheavals that have occurred in many provinces in Tonkin and other parts of Indochina as well, Hung Yen has been free from noisy demonstrations. Indeed, revolutionary elements cannot be recruited among those who till the land, shut off as they are in their native villages and solely concerned with the harvest and the produce from their rice fields. Lenin's followers seem to have realized this.

This was written in 1932 by the mandarin governor of Hung Yen in his report to the colonial authorities on the situation in his province. His conclusion stated:

> The Hung Yen peasant is still a tiller of the land, lacks any extraordinary stamina or enthusiasm, puts all his hopes and expectations into bumper crops, and entrusts his fate to the rain, wind and sun.

With this type of explanation, the colonial administration could set its mind at ease, keep collecting taxes and let mandarins and notables continue to exercise their privileges. Resigned to his lot in the face of the wind and rain, the peasant would be meek and submissive before the authorities. But the mandarin must have had his suspicions, because in his report he mentioned the history of some "bandits" who had given serious trouble to the French and mandarin troops during the last years of the nineteenth century:

> Bandits sprang up from everywhere. They used the reed swamps for refuge, which the soldiers could not penetrate. Invisible from the outside, the bandits were like tigers which hide behind bushes and jump out unexpectedly at their prey. Not one operation was undertaken without unfortunate losses.

The French administrator Miribel also recalled the history of these guerrillas who shook the province from 1883 to 1892, although it had been officially "conquered" by colonial troops on November 21, 1872 without a single shot having been fired:

> At the sight of the French soldiers, the Governor ordered the gates of the citadel to be opened. He gathered the mandarins of the province and ceremoniously went out to meet the French officers. All of them promised to be loyal to France.

If victory over the mandarins came so easily, the struggle with the "bandits" was a lot more difficult, because

> our military post did not know the country, could not get any information from the villages, and could not make any progress against the rebels, whose size and influence grew stronger day by day.

In fact, as Miribel acknowledged, the only information the French command ever got came from the European missionaries who were living in the countryside. Who were these "bandits"? Miribel described some of the leaders as follows:

> Tan Thuat and Cu Duc were the apostles. They visited the villages, got the notables together and inspired fervent patriotism in the hearts of everyone. Both these men were completely selfless and showed the greatest gentleness toward their fellow man. They preached resistance against the foreigner but tried to win over their partisans through persuasion rather than by terror.

Despite nine years of guerrilla warfare, the "bandits" of Hung Yen were forced to disperse after unrelenting pressure by French troops, aided by the mandarinate administration. For nine years, Hung Yen had been crisscrossed by a tight network of military posts.

History seemed to repeat itself half a century later. The French Expeditionary Corps reoccupied Hung Yen, strategically located in the heart of the Red River delta, as early as January 1947. Shortly thereafter, the provincial capital and the railway and Highway No. 5, two main arteries which cross the northern part of Hung Yen, and Highway No. 39, which crosses the province from top to bottom, were all retaken by the French. Fortified posts were set up at strategic points. Mandarins and notables, driven from their lands and privileged status by the Revolution in 1945-46, started to return. The French gave arms to the Catholic priests and missionaries to organize a Catholic militia; many churches were converted into blockhouses. French and "auxiliary" troops fanned out from the posts in sweep operations. Their main target was members of the Communist Party (renamed the Workers' Party in 1951) and members of the youth organization. In Dong Tao village, 42 young people were hanged on the branches of an ancient banyan tree. In Mai Xa, 12 Party members had their throats cut in the market place. Gradually, the colonialists established puppet village councils—"*te*" councils as the people called them—in almost all the villages. The noose on Party militants and resistance committees tightened day by day.

After their October 1950 defeat on the Chinese-Vietnamese border, the colonialists withdrew their forces to the delta provinces, trying at all costs to hold the line there, behind a string of bunkers called the De Lattre Line. Mop-up operations assumed proportions never before known. More and more blockhouses and watchtowers were built, and in 1951-52 there were 488 of them in Hung Yen alone. The years 1949-51 were terrible ones indeed, the present heads of the province tell us. Flat as a pancake and backed up against the river, Hung Yen could not offer its guerrilla fighters thick jungle hideouts and well-concealed caves, as did other provinces. The reed swamps which had sheltered Tan Thuat's "bandits" had disappeared and in any event would not have been of much use in an era of planes and helicopters. A single napalm bomb would have burned alive all the guerrillas. The order handed down to Party militants and resistance committees of Hung Yen instructed them: "Hold Hung Yen at all costs! Make Hung Yen a bastion in the enemy's rear!"

This order had to be carried out in the face of relentless mop-up operations and overflying aircraft, which could detect everything on the ground like hawks and could strafe at will. While the historic operations which would lead to Dien Bien Phu were being carried out beyond the delta, the delta provinces such as Hung Yen were supposed to pin down the greatest possible number of French and auxiliary troops. There were no forests or caves in these provinces, so underground hideouts of all shapes and sizes were dug. Sometimes you would have to dive into a pond to find the entrance. Wherever they were, the cadres could not go out during the day, and had to travel at night. When a big column of enemy troops arrived, people dispersed to the fields, leaving an empty village. Here and there a mine would explode under the feet of the aggressors, or a soldier would fall into a booby trap fitted with sharp spikes, or when they least expected it shots would come from nowhere, often with deadly precision. When they could, the French troops would destroy the village, or would have it razed to the ground by planes and artillery. Then they withdrew and shut themselves up in military posts. Gradually the guerrillas built up their armament; by 1953, Hung Yen guerrilla units were almost as well equipped as regular units. The French command had to deploy whole regiments for mop-up operations in which the Expeditionary Corps suffered heavier and heavier losses. Watchtowers maintained by auxiliary troops fell like autumn leaves, as did the larger fortified posts soon thereafter.

The Hung Yen peasant, whom the Mandarin Report described as lacking stamina, had become a tough guerrilla. No enemy movement escaped his vigilant eyes. While the French Expeditionary Corps operated blindly, the people's forces got all the information they needed, even inside the fortified posts held by the French. French troops massacred buffalo to starve out the people, who tilled their fields anyway with hoes and axes or harnessed themselves to their plows. The enemy tried to steal the ripened rice, but the people, protected by guerrillas and regular units, harvested the rice at night. In between enemy sweep operations, general education courses and political meetings were conducted, artistic performances given, and taxes collected.

But in order to intensify the guerrilla warfare, harvest the rice and prevent the people from being deceived by the *te* councils, the Party had to be there. It was the Party cadre who helped the people see clearly in the midst of the confusion and who taught them to analyze facts and events, and in so doing instilled confidence and courage in them. Whatever the risks, the Party cadre was always there.

Today, when you go to the province museum to see the first weapons the guerrillas used, their mimeograph machine for printing leaflets, the guitar which entertained them during their leisure moments (made from an empty biscuit can thrown away by French troops), you are tempted to smile at these things which seem more like toys than weapons. Remember, though, that by 1952-54, in the space of only a few years, Hung Yen guerrilla units had grown so strong that they were able to stand up to whole regiments of enemy troops supported by air power and artillery.

Hung Yen waged 9,022 battles from 1947 to 1954, in the course of which 19,200 enemy soldiers were killed and 15,000 captured. Four hundred eighty-four blockhouses and watchtowers were taken, 60 amphibious tanks, 544 trucks, two planes, two warboats, 52 locomotives and 154 railway carriages, and 5,400 rifles and 770 machine and submachine guns were taken from the enemy. The best of the French generals were powerless before these barefoot peasants.

A Bastion

Tam Nong village looks just like any other delta village, with its bamboo hedges, ponds, thatch-roofed huts, and rice fields. The details furnished to us by comrade Dao Thien, our guide and host, however, made us realize that nothing in this village was older than ten years, simply because everything had been completely destroyed by French planes and artillery during the war. "These bamboo groves, those Japanese lilac trees," he said, "were all planted after peace came. Behind this clump of bamboo was the entrance to one of my underground caches; I had six in all. A trench started along this embankment, which we used as a communications line during combat operations. That pond over there used to be a bomb crater . . . . " The real picture of the village became even clearer after comrade Thien told us the story about the relentless struggle which had lasted many years here.

"I was nineteen," he said, "when I joined the youth group in 1944. Why did I join? To fight the French and follow the 'communists'? I didn't know what communism meant; all I knew was that the French would be driven out and the poor would have their own rice fields. As early as 1942, the whole village had been stirred up by the news that two peasants had shoved a sign reading, 'Down with Exorbitant Taxes!' in front of the car of a French official who had come down to inspect the province. In 1944, we stormed the depots where the Japanese stored the rice, to distribute it to the people. We took power in 1945, but that was also the year of the great famine. The Party gave top priority to national unity in the struggle against the colonialists, so we left the property of the rich untouched. We merely asked them to contribute rice to a relief fund, which many of them did. On the local level we carried out the policy of the National Front. But the rice fields belonging to landowners who had fled to the towns seeking protection by French troops were distributed to the poor peasants. Revolutionary power was set up in our village and we enlisted in a guerrilla unit. We had no rifles yet. But in 1947, when the enemy occupied the northern part of our province, our guerrillas went as far as the Hanoi-Haiphong railway line 21 miles away to participate in engagements there and gain combat experience.

"In 1948, the enemy widened its zone of occupation. Some enemy troops quartered themselves in the church in Lay village, a few miles from here, showering bullets on us from time to time. In June 1948, our provincial units staged a battle in Thi marketplace, three miles away from here. We started to fortify the village and lay mines. Money was collected for arms and mines during weddings and other family ceremonies. But we still didn't have any good rifles, let alone submachine guns. This situation, however, did not stop us from writing this inscription on the walls of our village: 'We shall launch an all-out counteroffensive on

December 19, 1949!'[12] Three days later a strong enemy column entered and occupied the village for 24 hours. We didn't have enough rifles to fight back so the guerrillas dispersed, most of them hiding behind the bamboo hedges. The Party Provincial Committee had previously instructed us to dig underground hideouts, but we had neglected to do so, thinking the enemy would never come as far as our village. Fortunately, the enemy troops themselves didn't have much experience with mop-up operations. They rounded up some women and old people, beat them and shouted, 'So this is your all-out counteroffensive!' They even wrote on our walls: 'Launching an all-out counteroffensive for you means runnings scared in front of the French mandarins!'

"After the enemy left, we called a meeting to see what lessons we could draw from this initial contact. We dug new hideouts, strengthened the fortified defenses of the village, and carefully studied the paths leading in and out of the village before we laid our mines and traps. The Provincial Committee sent us six rifles and lots of mines. As for the inscription left by the enemy, we added: 'We'll see who'll be running scared!' Some of our militants, however, were apprehensive and asked to be sent to the liberated areas. So a district unit with a light machine gun was sent down to reinforce us.

"By mid-1950, I don't quite remember the exact day, another enemy column returned on a mop-up operation. The machine gun was hidden in a cache dug in the yard of a house which was set on fire by the enemy. Some of our comrades who were in the dugout couldn't stand the terrible heat and came out with the gun, firing on the enemy. Two of them were killed and the machine gun was lost, but some of the enemy soldiers were killed by our mines and booby traps.

"Again, we drew lessons from the engagement. We moved our underground caches away from the dwellings, dug

[11] The third anniversary of the launching of the war of liberation on a national scale.

communication trenches to crisscross the whole village, and widened our network of mines and traps. I myself dug six different underground hideouts. We obtained 18 rifles and hundreds of mines. In the beginning of 1951, the enemy started its big sweep operations to 'pacify' the delta. Six battalions assigned to raid the region attacked our village. As usual, everyone evacuated the village and only the fighters remained. Our network of mines and traps was so good that enemy soldiers fell at each step along the way. The first mine to explode killed a French lieutenant. They were only able to advance at a snail's pace along narrow paths. Our snipers, hidden behind fortifications, were waiting for them and shot them down one by one, hitting the mark almost every time. The enemy launched five successive attacks, but failed in all five, suffering 25 casualties. We lost one comrade. At nightfall, the enemy withdrew.

"Another onslaught was expected. We told the population to evacuate the village and seek refuge in neighboring villages where *te* councils had been set up by the enemy and hence were not subject to bombing. The people left, but returned in the daytime to work in the fields. Only the guerrillas and Party members stayed behind. A few days later, 25 planes came over the village and dropped napalm and bombs all over it. All the houses were destroyed, but the guerrillas, hidden in fortifications and underground shelters, waited for the enemy. When the French troops advanced, thinking the bombing had reduced our forces to nothing, they were surprised to be received by heavy fire. They gave up that attempt.

"Then we received a visit from a Party provincial leader, who ordered us to evacuate the village temporarily, hide our weapons and lay a thick mine field. His order was carried out that very night. The following day the enemy made another attack, preceded by intense artillery fire. The enemy troops advanced very slowly, suffering heavy casualties because of the mines. They caught one of our men and by horrible torture got the information out of him that our forces had been evacuated. They entered the village and occupied it for 15 days, destroying everything. To sow discord they authorized people in neighboring villages to come and plunder whatever they could lay their hands on. When they left, the village was a heap of ruins soon to be taken over by weeds and undergrowth. The population had dispersed into neighboring communities. The Party decided that the guerrillas should come back and reoccupy the village to instill confidence in the people, and to create a fortified base in the enemy's rear.

"Nine Party members came back, cleared out some ground and built a few huts. We encouraged the people to return and cultivate the land, while continuing to live in neighboring villages. One of the latter had a *te* council, but we talked its members into helping us and serving as a cover. The great victories won by the People's Army had a profound influence among those who had put themselves in the service of the enemy. In the last years of the war, we sometimes even hid in the houses of notables who collaborated with the enemy. We once intercepted a supply convoy being sent to Bao Dai[13] troops; a single shot dispersed the entire escort. The booty gave our forces provisions for many weeks, and we even distributed gifts to the population, whose morale was growing all the time.

"From 1953 to 1954 we fought enemy troops each time they undertook a mop-up raid in our region, but they no longer singled out our village for attack. A circle of high grass had grown up alongside the fortifications around the village, which caused great fear among the French and auxiliary troops, because one of our men had been fatally bitten there by a poisonous snake customarily found in this type of undergrouth. After the news spread, no enemy soldier dared come near the village for fear of being bitten. The population gradually regained confidence and came back to rebuild the village. In the last months of the war, we finally came out of

[13]Bao Dai was the Vietnamese king installed by the French.—*Ed.*

hiding and our fortified positions to pursue enemy units known as M.G.'s (Mobile Groups), which earlier had sown terror among the populace on the plains.

"In all, we fought 226 battles and killed 362 enemy soldiers. Our village was awarded the Resistance Order, First Class."

From Guerrilla Unit to Technical School

In the period immediately following the war, Hung Yen was in a wretched state because it lacked modern equipment. Nevertheless, the guerrilla war of 1947 to 1954, waged on a much larger scale than that of 1883 and against a much more powerful enemy, had produced some valuable assets: thousands of Party militants, tens of thousands of guerrilla fighters, and a population in which everyone directly or indirectly had participated in the war. Land reform, conducted from 1954 to 1957, was no less an important upheaval in social, economic and psychological terms. During 1958 another milestone was achieved: the eradication of illiteracy, which had afflicted 95 percent of the population and against which a determined struggle had been waged even during the war.

Victory over a modern army equipped with powerful weapons, victory over age-old feudalism, victory over ignorance: this threefold victory gave the people, especially the poor peasantry, great confidence in their own strength and almost limitless confidence in the Party which led them. The Party Committee of Hung Yen assessed the situation in these terms during its November 1956 meeting which launched the great agricultural cooperativization campaign:

> First, the favorable factors are:
> —There is a good attitude on the part of the cadres, Party members and the population as a whole as a result of the rectification of the errors committed during the land reform program and the campaign against drought.

—The resistance and land reform carried out under the leadership of the Party have educated the population in a spirit of heroic struggle and labor and have given them absolute confidence in the Party.

—The peasants have begun to realize that collective labor is necessary, as a result of the struggle against drought.

—A fixed limit to the agricultural tax has given the peasants more confidence in the Party.

—The harvest has been good, and the time is ripe to launch the campaign.

—The three pilot cooperatives have been successful and well received by the population.

—The local Party leaders have become closer to the masses as a result of the rectification of errors campaign after the land reform and as a result of the struggle against drought. One hundred and eleven section secretaries, 282 deputy secretaries and 2,020 Party members have taken courses on how to advance from mutual aid teams to cooperatives. This has been critical for the cooperativization campaign.

The unfavorable factors and difficulties are as follows:

—Provincial and district cadres have had no direct experience in setting up coops.

—The various needs of coops being set up are important, but the different branches serving these coops have had no direct experience in the problems involved.

—Problems involved in lands where the owners are absent (those gone to the South) or which belong to Catholic missions are quite complex, since they are related to different policies.

—We have had little experience and have not been able to draw lessons from previous work. The masses want the leadership to give them a clear direction and concrete knowledge, but the leadership's capacities are still limited. If we are not careful, the movement will either take on a spontaneous, directionless character, or we will slow it down.

However, the difficulties are only temporary, and the favorable factors are basically the main elements in the situation.

The masses wanted the leadership to provide them with the ability and knowledge which comes only from experience, but this leadership comprised a mere handful of provincial leaders and a few thousand Party militants scattered throughout the villages. So, Hung Yen had to start a major new battle—a stepped-up campaign to train new cadres. In the space of a few years 1,000 coop leaders and 3,500 heads of production teams took courses for two or more weeks, either in the provincial capital or in the district centers. Hundreds of accountants were trained. All types of educational techniques were used. When an exhibition on the agricultural achievements of the People's Republic of China was organized in Hanoi, focusing on improved farm implements, Hung Yen mobilized 8,000 people to go see it. When a cooperative in a neighboring province or in Hung Yen itself was particularly successful in one field or another, cadres of other coops came to visit it. This province which didn't have a single newpaper under the colonial regime now buys 3,000 copies of each issue of the magazine *Practical Science*, which features articles on applied agronomy. Another innovation is that bookshops sell books and brochures on growing rice and corn and on coop management. There are now 1,900 book collections belonging to the province's cooperatives, villages, schools and youth groups—each counting several hundred titles. Thien Thang village is the proud owner of a 3,000-book library. Books are publicized by teams traveling from one village to the next.

The villages have set up song and drama groups to perform short plays featuring various "positive" and "negative" characters who emerged in the course of the cooperativization campaign. All these plays required were a few wooden boards, a gasoline lamp, everyday clothing, no curtain or stage wings, stage characters typical of people one meets in everyday life, and scenes and words drawn from work sessions, discussions and games. The plays drew much laughter and excitement from people because they led them to relive some of the episodes in their own past. *Indictment against the Underground Dragon* was a play that dealt with the digging of a canal. *Whose Fault Was It?* exposed the mistakes committed by a management committee. *The Re-*

volt of the Buffalo denounced those who neglected coop buffalo under their supervision. About 200 amateur groups in Hung Yen performed in these plays.

Villages also built new schools and conducted supplementary courses for adults who had already learned to read and write. Hung Yen had 130,000 children in school. Out of a total of 156 villages in the province, 102 had junior high schools (through the seventh grade[14]); the 54 remaining villages all had four-grade primary schools. There were six senior high schools in Hung Yen, taking students through the tenth grade. Seventy-five percent of the village cadres attained an educational level equivalent to that of fifth grade, and one-fourth of them had taken the seventh grade examinations and had received their diplomas.

Cadres in the province were mostly of poor peasant origin. Poor peasants constituted 66 percent of the Party membership, and out of 156 village Party secretaries, 105 were poor peasants. There were 17 agricultural schools in the province which taught elementary agricultural techniques. A high school-level agricultural school was set up in December 1961, and we visited this school.

Peasant members of cooperatives having at least one year's agricultural work to their credit were admitted to the school. They were sent by their coops, to which they returned at the end of their 18-month period of study. The purpose of the school was to teach the students basic agricultural techniques and give them a minimal level of theory so that they could apply the techniques without becoming real experts.

There were three main areas of study: crops, animal husbandry and aquatic products. The school was opened even before the buildings had been erected. Classes were held in an experimental station building and the students stayed in the homes of people in the neighborhood. Despite

[14]There are ten grades in the North Vietnamese elementary and secondary school system.—*Ed.*

these conditions, 185 students enrolled during the first year and studied under two recently graduated engineers and five technical cadres. Students and teachers helped out in the construction of school buildings, which are now nearly completed.

The director received us in a small room that served as both his office and his personal quarters. Neither the room nor the furniture had anything "directorial" about them, and the director's bike, which he used to get around the province, was in one corner of the room. In the courtyard could be seen two types of students: peasants over 30 years of age in their traditional brown outfits, and younger people in blue or khaki shirts, also peasants but one generation younger. The first class of graduates, which completed the course in the summer of 1963, included a high proportion of middle-aged peasants, and over half of the graduates were Party members. The average educational level of the students was fifth grade. In 1962 and 1963 the student body included a higher proportion of young people, and their educational level rose to the seventh grade. The director told us:

"The most difficult thing is to inculcate in the students basic scientific knowledge, such as chemistry, plant and animal physiology. Half the time is devoted to theoretical studies. All of our students have had practical experience, since only peasants sent by their coops, and not liberal arts graduates, are enrolled here. Needless to say, our school has its own garden, pigsty, experimental fields and silkworm breeding room, but the students often go to the coops in the neighborhood to do field work. We're trying to increase production on our own fields to meet our needs. How much will our graduates be paid when they finish school? Will they be paid by the state or the province? Will they be satisfied with the same amount that other members of their coops are paid, which is calculated according to the amount of work done? Well, there are different opinions on these questions. All we know is that after they graduate they return to the coops from which they came. In just a few years from now, each coop will have at least one technician who has been trained in our school. Young people have already set up scientific and technical study groups in many coops, and supplemental courses on agriculture have been given regularly for some time."

From Dream to Reality

We rode along the dike of the Luoc River, then along the Peace Canal, accompanied by the president of the Administrative Committee of the province. Sampans glided up the river, their sales billowing as they carried jute, bananas and geese from Hung Yen to Haiphong or brought coal and cement back to the province. The waters had receded on the other side of the dike, exposing a wide stretch of the bank, which numerous work teams were engaged in repairing. A canal, a sluice gate, and, on this side of the dike, ripening rice fields. "Rice in November, " said the president. "People here have been dreaming of this for centuries, because this area is barely three feet above sea level. During the rainy season it used to be a veritable lake, and it was impossible to transplant a single rice seedling the whole summer. Now, with the canals and sluices, enough of the water can be drained out so that the rice fields produce at least two harvests a year. Moreover (pointing), we're going to build a new electric pumping station here." Then without pausing he added, "Over there you can see where we fought against the tanks."

We asked him, "Why are those isolated houses sitting in the middle of the rice fields?" It is rare to find in the Vietnamese countryside houses huddled together on elevated tracts of land in the middle of flooded rice fields.

"During the war," he answered, "when the French bombed our villages, some of the people preferred to build their huts right in the middle of the rice fields."

We crossed some fields where the rice was riper than elsewhere. The president said, "Look at the small dikes, they are all straight and several hundred yards long. These fields have been plowed by tractors, so they could be planted with seedlings earlier than the others. We don't have many tractors yet, maybe 50 in the whole province. In fact, mechanization here is first used in water conservation work rather than in plowing." Water conservation not only supplies water to the rice fields but has also freed people's shoulders from heavy loads, which are now carried up the canal on small boats made of bamboo and laden with sugar cane and bricks.

"When we had to live in underground hideouts," said the president, "we often dreamed about what the future would be like. We knew that one day we would have socialism, but we could scarcely imagine what that would mean in concrete terms." Then he told us about a battle that had taken place on the bridge we were crossing. The land here is as full of history as it is of men's projects for the future. The dream of the mandarin in 1932 came to our minds: all the water needed would be available for the rice fields, rice would abound in plenty, the number of wrongdoers would decrease, more and more public services would be available. We also thought of the pitiful beggars who used to swarm along the roads and marketplaces, assailing travelers, giving Hung Yen a national reputation. Whenever someone was particularly annoying, people would say, "You whine like a Khoai Chau beggar!" Today, after traveling all over Hung Yen, we have not seen a single person holding out his hand. During the time when the mandarin was dreaming, there were only 5,750 school pupils in the whole province, and now there are 130,000. Movies were previously unknown to Hung Yen peasants, but by 1962 people were seeing an average of two to three films a year. Eight traveling teams were going all over the province to show Vietnamese, Soviet, Chinese, Romanian and Bulgarian films. Of course, we are not yet in a land of plenty; our daily diet of rice, meat and fish is still a far cry from that eaten by an American. Now all children attend school, and nobody, absolutely nobody, is left to starve on the road even when there is a long spell of drought or when typhoons swoop down on the province. Let

us repeat that there are no more beggars in this province, that
the Hung Yen peasant with his plot of land has recovered his
dignity, and that he is protected in his cooperative from
natural disasters, which may still rob him of some food but
can no longer starve him. Under socialism, the Hung Yen
peasant has achieved *security*.

Along the way, we met an old peasant woman who
invited us over to her house. As we entered her courtyard the
president of the Provincial Committee—in the old days he
would have been called the mandarin governor—drew a
bucket of water from the well to wash the mud off his feet.
Before he poured the water on his feet he let the old woman
have some first. His gesture called to mind a not-too-distant
past, when a visit from the mandarin governor would have
brought him to the village suitably attired in ceremonial
costume, transported in a swaying palanquin, preceded by
arrogant guards, peasants bowing down as he passed, not even
daring to look up at him.

*   *   *   *   *

It was raining hard the day we left Tien Tien, the last
village we visited. We had to push our bikes along the muddy,
slippery paths for miles on end. The peasants were lifting up
one by one the ripened rice ears which had fallen into the
water because of the rain. Yes, peasant life in Hung Yen is
still hard, but you can hear them singing:

"We have conquered the colonialists and we're going to
conquer heaven too!"

"To conquer heaven"—no one would have dared utter
such a blasphemy even 15 years ago. To conquer heaven the
people of Hung Yen will need more machinery and industry.
The province is still behind others in terms of improved farm
implements, and hoeing, plowing and canal-dredging are still
done with old tools. A small machine shop has been
built in the provincial capital and we know that the provincial leaders have dreams of expanding it.

On this land, the era of the colonialists and the mandarins has ended. The dream is already beginning to be the reality.

The Vietnamese Experience and the Third World

Based on Vietnam's experience over the past years, I wish to make some general observations about development in the third world. The major consideration, though not the sole one, for my treating such a topic is undoubtedly my own participation in the Vietnamese experience and my personal familiarity with many of the aspects involved. Furthermore, the historical process has moved so fast over the past years in Vietnam that my country has passed rapidly through a succession of different phases. Over a period of 15 years, an adult would have lived under totally different social, political and economic regimes, directly experiencing such important movements as a war of national liberation, land reform, and the transition from a colonial and feudal regime to an independent and finally socialist state.

Ideological Liberation

First, some way must be found to measure underdevelopment. People sometimes talk about the "horse and buggy" era in the West in order to evoke memories of a distant past. Vietnam at present has not even reached the horse and buggy age. Over winding country paths people still carry all their food and belongings on their shoulders, and a wheelbarrow represents a technological innovation. Vietnam is technologically some 300 years behind Europe. When French technicians were withdrawn in 1955, the government of the Democratic Republic of Vietnam had available only about 30 engineers. The French geographer, Pierre Gourou, who knew the country well, characterized it as a "vegetable civilization" where even the smallest steel nail was imported.

This technical backwardness meant general underdevelopment in all sectors. In 1955, studies involving 80,000 people showed that 80 percent of the population living in the lowlands had trachoma.[1] Many peasants still did not dare to sink wells, even shallow ones, for fear of wounding the subterranean dragon. Many families still forced their young daughters to marry between the ages of 12 and 15.

What steps has North Vietnam taken to solve these problems of underdevelopment? An agronomist, if asked,

---

[1] Trachoma is a contagious disease found in tropical climates, and is characterized by a chronic inflammation of the eyelids.—*Ed.*

This article was first published in early 1961 and was reprinted in Expériences Vietnamiennes, *Nguyen Khac Vien (Paris: Editions Sociales, 1971). A few passages have been overtaken by events and are thus omitted. The basic argument, however, remains as topical as ever.*

would say that agricultural progress depends on the application of new agricultural techniques: increased irrigation, deeper plowing, more manure, and tighter transplanting, all of which is true enough. An economist would stress fundamental principles of economic development. He would say, for example, that the government of the Democratic Republic of Vietnam was wise in concentrating its efforts simultaneously on industry and local trade. Or that it was wise to undertake both major and minor irrigation projects with particular emphasis on those not requiring a high level of investment; or to impose strict controls over imports, while prohibiting all luxury goods from entering the country in order to concentrate on heavy machinery and equipment; or to eliminate all superfluous expenditures. These are undoubtedly basic principles.

Yet all these explanations fail to answer one question: why have other governments been unable to exploit adequately the same methods or profit from the advice of enlightened economists?

To find the most appropriate type of plow or the best way to transplant rice is relatively easy. Furthermore, it is common knowledge that if all the manure and human waste scattered about in the villages were collected, a good source of fertilizer would become immediately available, and a major source of disease checked. It is far better to make this type of operation succeed than to import tons of antibiotics. If each peasant were to make his own small wheelbarrow with a wooden wheel instead of carrying everything on his back, transportation capacity would quickly double without having to wait until trucks could be acquired.

This leads us to the crux of the matter: *if each peasant* collected fertilizer, *if each peasant* changed the blade on his plow, and so on . . . . Technicians may draw up blueprints, economists may formulate plans, and the government may legislate, but how can millions of peasants learn overnight how to change the blade on their plows and how to modify their old method of transplanting rice?

In answer to this question, the North Vietnamese experience shows that a double-pronged campaign of "rectification" and "emulation" must be waged against every major problem of economic development. What does the term "rectification" mean, and why does it alarm so many people? Simply stated, it means nothing more than holding discussion meetings at all levels where everyone can air his or her daily problems. Some of the matters discussed center on why cooperatives are created, why thrift is necessary, why a particular rule exists, why we are producing, how we produce, why polygamy and child marriage are forbidden. In the course of these meetings, people study and examine governmental instructions in detail, word by word, sentence by sentence. Everyone has an opportunity to speak. Each person will criticize the others' ideas or will in turn have his ideas criticized so that any errors can be corrected.

North Vietnam is a country where people are very talkative. In every factory, cooperative, agency and neighborhood, large and small meetings are constantly being held. In order to overcome underdevelopment, you cannot mince words.

Rectification campaigns on all levels are always undertaken before any other projects get underway. As Marx said, "Once ideas filter down to the consciousness of the masses, they become a material force."

Once ideas have been corrected and the new ones properly implemented, the emulation campaign begins. Within a short time, obscure peasants can become famous throughout the country because they have found the best way to breed water buffalo or because they have collected so many tons of fertilizer. The names of the innovators are on everyone's lips. Our magazines are filled with stories about the innovations of peasants and workers, rather than the romance of some fairy princess or the exploits of some gangster. Concrete personal experiences become precise standards which guide all efforts on the individual level.

Emulation campaigns also occur on the group level. A

particular farm cooperative or mining team may be honored, such as the Dai Phong Cooperative which successfully developed local trade along with its agriculture and now serves as a model for all other cooperatives. Work methods are carefully studied everywhere. What is being done at the Duyen Hai factory is discussed in all other factories.

Vivid slogans bring home the principles embodied in these emulation campaigns. To induce people to make wheelbarrows, the political slogan, "Free your shoulders," is used. To stimulate the campaign to clear land for farming: "Break the chains of the one-tenth hectare" (the one-tenth hectare available to each person). For manure and garbage collection: "Clean villages mean well-manured rice land."

Rectification and emulation campaigns encourage the use of many new initiatives. When you are 300 years behind the times, the smallest daily acts have to be changed, and the work of each moment modified if modernization is to be achieved. Everything, in fact, has to be changed regardless of whether it is the shape of a plane or a saw, the method used to sink wells or build a road, learning how to run a small factory, the use of screws or ball bearings. The creation of a few modern centers does not solve the problem.

A country can either find the way to encourage the development of constant initiative among its common people, thus facilitating rapid development, or it can neglect this resource and thus condemn itself both to slow growth and, what is worse, to social turmoil for years to come.

Dare to think about progress, dare to take initiative, dare to transform your ideas into reality. This is the general political slogan which now inspires all North Vietnam. An underdeveloped country is essentially a feudal and precapitalist society which totally excludes any ideas about progress. The members of such a society are afraid to change, whether they be peasants, tradesmen or members of the upper classes. Each action and mannerism is above all a rite which cannot be modified for any reason. Society is carefully arranged into a hierarchy according to a supernaturally inspired plan.

Contrary to the illusory, superficial activity seething among some segments of the urban populace, until recently the great majority of the people were untouched by the idea of progress. Yet it is these people, immobilized by the age-old traditions of an extremely hierarchical society, who must be awakened before any kind of development can occur, and it is they who must be persuaded that social customs, modes of living, and work methods can and must be changed.

The following example illustrates the burden of feudal ideology. Tradition required that after the death of a parent, the children had to abstain from all public activity for at least three years. Toward the beginning of the twentieth century, the great scholar and patriot, Phan Boi Chau,[2] was yearning to enter the struggle for independence and the modernization of his country. He had the misfortune to lose his mother just when he was about to embark on his revolutionary calling. He waited three years before beginning his public career. So it should be no surprise if similar taboos, implicit or explicit, have a paralyzing effect on simple, illiterate peasants, inhibiting all progress. Ideological liberation of the great majority of the people is the *sine qua non* of development. There is no question that for developing countries, liberty is the most precious of all blessings—not the negative liberty which demands "leave me alone," but a true liberation of spirit and energy.

Underdeveloped countries need *first and foremost an ideology of progress* which is able to mobilize, organize and educate their people. The worst enemy of progress is any kind of excessive religious belief which paralyzes the common people. No less pernicious are the use of empiricism and short-sighted solutions which inhibit the development of a broader outlook. The human spirit is not nourished on ingenious stratagems and clever propositions.

[2] For further discussion of Phan Boi Chau and his scholar-patriot contemporaries, see David G. Marr, *Vietnamese Anticolonialism, 1885-1925*, Berkeley: University of California Press, 1971.—*Ed.*

Land Reform: An Anti-feudal Revolution

Yet, are we to believe that progress can only be accomplished through the intensive use of propaganda and education? It is not because speeches have been made nor because pamphlets have been distributed that the mass of the Vietnamese people have changed, but rather because life itself has made them change. The war they were forced to confront from 1945 to 1954 awakened the most distant hamlets from their torpor. For the first time in their lives, millions of peasants left their villages, some enlisting in the People's Army, some carrying supplies to the troops, others fleeing from regions devastated by bombing and mop-up operations. New social contacts dissolved the traditional hierarchy and made the ritual of daily life impossible. Year after year, the war required a growing contribution of manpower, materiel and provisions. Peasants, who made up nine-tenths of the population, provided the major support for the war. Toward the end of the conflict, we could not simply promise them national independence without giving them a clear idea of what this entailed. In 1953 they had to be given their own land.

The struggle for national independence brought about the overthrow of an agrarian structure which had been passed down unchanged for centuries. Land reform was a compelling necessity.

When the war ended and the severe problems of economic development had to be faced, the land reform program was still not finished. The distribution of land to the peasantry was actually the only way to create a domestic market capable of stimulating industrial development.

Economic experts from the United Nations have been known to amuse themselves by lavishing advice on governments of developing countries, recommending this or that formula for land reform. As if it were a question of a simple economic technique! As if it were enough to formulate sound laws and leave their enforcement in the hands of efficient bureaucrats! Do not forget that underdeveloped countries are characterized by inefficient centralized bureaucracies, and that power is entrenched in local feudal principalities which are controlled by landowners and village notables, as a result of age-old traditions. The best of laws passed by a central government will remain a dead letter if they conflict with the interests of the local oligarchy. In these countries, no government possesses an adequate army of able and loyal bureaucrats capable of breaking this resistance. Reforms are likely to be swallowed up by the centuries-old bog of feudalism.

The first condition for radical land reform is the complete overthrow of the existing social and political structures. Feudal resistance can only be broken by complete mobilization of the peasant masses. North Vietnam found it necessary to replace the old village administrations one by one, mobilizing the peasants in each village and launching the struggle against the power held by landowners and notables.

Above all else, land reform is an *anti-feudal revolution.* It has been a great test for North Vietnam and represents an historical experience as profound as—if not more than—the war of national liberation. It could not have taken place in so short a time if the peasantry had not been mobilized and if a profound ideological revolution had not shaken the peasant mentality. The fact that poor, illiterate peasants have dared to form administrative committees replacing the old village oligarchy, without fear of the wrath of heaven or the gods, is an historical change the consequences of which are still being felt.

Participation in the struggle for national independence was the first step toward the awakening of millions of poor and resigned peasants. It facilitated the formation of class consciousness and made the working peasantry more aware of its specific class interests, in opposition to those of landlords and notables. The peasantry consequently became increasingly patriotic.

This twofold raising of consciousness on the part of the

peasant masses is what I believe to be an essential and indispensable condition for rapid progress. Land reform must be conducted by means of an incisive class struggle. Land distribution is certainly the basic objective, although feudal structures must also be destroyed and impoverished peasants made aware of their own interests.

The peasant revolution in North Vietnam intensified the national struggle, stimulated heroic efforts during the last year of the war, and at the same time laid the groundwork for future development. Without land reform, there would not have been a Dien Bien Phu.

Among developing countries, it is easy to distinguish those which have successfully carried out radical land reform programs and those which either did not undertake them or have been satisfied with a mere semblance of reform. In the first case, the peasants are new people, ready to seize the initiative; in the second, they have remained as they have been for centuries, resigned and slaves to the habits of the past.

An Historic Decision: Capitalism or Socialism?

With national independence secured, land reform was completed in North Vietnam by 1956 and the country was free to choose its own road to progress. The essential question remained, however: which road should be chosen? How could we channel all the energy generated by the war of national liberation and the land reform movement? Should we rely on the free enterprise system, allowing each shopkeeper and small factory owner to run his own business as he saw fit and leaving to each peasant the responsibility of working his own plot of land? This would have been the capitalist route.

The Vietnamese bourgeoisie, however, was particularly underdeveloped. No capitalist firm had reached the point where it employed more than a hundred workers. In underdeveloped countries, the bourgeoisie is primarily commercial in nature. The most profitable business is importing watches, pens, textiles, drugs, bicycles, and luxuries for resale. Leaving the bourgeoisie to its own devices would have led to the extinction of any domestic industry.

Furthermore, accelerated industrial development requires the rapid formation of a skilled working class. Coolies or peasants newly arrived in the cities must be quickly trained as skilled workers. A worker might master his trade in three or four years, or within six months, depending upon the extent to which he is dedicated to his job. Hundreds of thousands of workers must be constantly innovative if a modern society with a climate favoring industrial development is to be created. People must also be willing to learn and assimilate in a short period of time a body of scientific and technical knowledge.

It is useless to install modern equipment in a factory if those who run it are unskilled and are politically unaware. This is especially true in a tropical climate where machines quickly deteriorate. Thus, rectification and emulation campaigns must be constantly held in the factories. Technology is not the sole concern of rectification programs, however, since techniques of management, administration and "human relations" are likewise frequent subjects for reexamination. The people who come to the meetings during these campaigns include workers who have in many cases taken an active part in the struggle for national liberation, as well as newly-arrived peasants who have already participated in the land reform movement. These people cannot be restricted to technical problems alone and excluded from the problems of management. In a capitalist company, however, it is unlikely that local party leaders or cadres would participate in actual labor or that workers would be involved in management. Similarly, it is most unlikely that capitalist companies would encourage continual rectification and emulation campaigns to encourage workers and managers.

It is possible that a particularly enterprising bourgeois class could be responsible for its country's industrialization.

This type of industrialization would call for a rather lengthy period during which the working class is resigned to its condition and during which any overseas colonies are exploited. Otherwise, the domestic market of the country in question must be exclusively in the hands of its national bourgeoisie, free of foreign competition. At present, however, none of these options is available to the Vietnamese bourgeoisie.

The capitalist solution for modernizing agriculture would require an even longer time. A half acre of rice-producing land is allotted to each peasant family in Vietnam. Modern methods cannot be applied to farms of this size, and even traditional irrigation methods meet insurmountable difficulties. Farm cooperatives comprising several hundred families must therefore be established if agriculture is to be modernized. In addition, farm cooperatives must promote both handicrafts and small industry so that jobs may be provided for everyone. The underemployment of millions of peasants can only be corrected by actively promoting these kinds of farm cooperatives.

Those who know Vietnamese peasants are astounded to see them in 1961 as leaders of cooperatives planning the construction of kilns and carpentry shops next to their rice silos, or planning the purchase of a tractor or a motor boat to transport rice. Only a few years ago such leaders were still humble peasants, bowed under the yoke of feudalism, illiterate, resigned to their condition and easy prey to famine and tropical diseases.

It is just as incredible that 40 miners from Hong Gai graduated this year as mining engineers from the Polytechnic Institute in Hanoi. Only a few years ago these miners were illiterate. Moreover, several thousand workers and peasants, completely free of material worries for themselves and their families, are now studying to enter the university through self-improvement courses.

None of this would have been possible had Vietnam chosen the capitalist route. Only socialism is able to create the necessary conditions to give free rein to the creative spirit of the people. Prime Minister Nehru spoke of a "feeling of frustration" which has taken hold of the Indian people since independence and is paralyzing that country's development. Capitalism is simply incapable of generating enthusiasm, at least among millions of workers and peasants.

A further distinction, therefore, must now be made between those underdeveloped countries which have chosen socialism (China, North Vietnam, North Korea) and those which have not. This leads us to the next question: which social class will lead this great movement?

The Question of Leadership

This is by no means a theoretical question. In Vietnam the bourgeoisie and the parties associated with it failed completely to regain national independence. The colonial repression which followed the abortive insurrection of 1930 decimated the bourgeois or petty bourgeois political groups. Only the Communist Party,[3] with deep roots among the people, survived this major repression to become *de facto* the sole leader of the national struggle. The protracted war of national liberation finally removed the remnants of the bourgeois parties or at least removed them from the leadership of events. Bourgeois political movements were not strong enough to solve and overcome problems of this magnitude.

Bourgeois movements are led primarily by those who come from intellectual and business circles. They lack a popular base in the mines, plantations, factories, to say nothing of the peasantry. The apologists of such movements, trained in Western-style universities, are undoubtedly capable of drawing up beautiful plans, writing constitutions, and making speeches at the United Nations; they are, however, totally incapable of organizing a strike, working for years on end in mines or on plantations, waging guerrilla warfare for

---

[3] Renamed the Vietnam Workers' Party in 1951.—*Ed.*

decades, or plodding through the mud of rice paddies.

The first directive issued by the Communist Party in Vietnam shortly after its founding ordered its political activists to work in the mines, become rickshaw pullers and to live and work among the peasants—to build a solid base of support among the people. Bourgeois politicians, on the other hand, spent their time primarily in contacting other politicians, journalists and foreign governments. Being city people by birth and education, they were unfamiliar with their own country, never having shared the life of the nine-tenths of the Vietnamese population who are poor peasants.

A bourgeois movement could possibly succeed if a country achieves independence without too great a struggle, either through negotiation or by compromise with the occupying power. When a protracted war of liberation must be waged, however, and the people mobilized for many long years, proponents of bourgeois ideology have to be disregarded.

Furthermore, the bourgeoisie in underdeveloped countries is so closely linked to the landowning class that it is incapable of promoting radical land reform. Numerous store and factory owners hold land in their own right and almost all of them are at least distantly related to the gentry. Peasant mobilization as it occurred in North Vietnam from 1953 to 1956 would be unthinkable under bourgeois leadership.

Nevertheless, assuming that a country is independent, could the bourgeoisie be counted on to implement the emulation and rectification campaigns throughout the population that are so necessary for rapid growth?

I doubt it. Simply because rectification and emulation campaigns involving an entire population require collective organization, as well as leaders trained to be sensitive to the needs of the masses. A tight group of political activists in each factory, village and district must be willing to share the common life of the masses, to recognize their aspirations, suggestions and reactions and to lead them into action.

What do the people want? What are they capable of doing at a given time or about a given problem? These questions are continually being raised in countries undergoing rapid change. To launch a movement of this type, there must be a determined vanguard of activists who will set an example, lead others into action, and explain as needed to the confused. Furthermore, it should be emphasized that not everyone is a friend of progress. The resistance of opponents must be broken at each step of the way.

Every rectification campaign must necessarily include the following steps: polling public opinion, educating the people, implementing tasks, eliminating reactionary elements by political means, and self-criticism by political activists. The following example illustrates this process. A health team arrived in a village with the mission of sinking a well so that the residents would no longer use a large pond for their drinking water. Some time thereafter, the inhabitants filled the well and returned to using the pond. Why did this happen and what should have been done?

Health team leaders and political activists from the local Workers' Party met to analyze the situation. It was not only a failure in terms of hygiene but represented a political failure as well. The health team was strongly criticized for acting in a "bureaucratic" manner in that it had perceived only the technical side of its work. Equipped with its knowledge and tools, it had proceeded to sink the well without bothering to educate the populace or encourage its participation. The people watched in open-mouthed admiration without understanding the reasons for it.

Unfortunately, some time later a local family lost a child to a mysterious illness. It was rumored that the death was the fault of the well, that the underground dragon was taking its revenge against the people. The villagers hastened one night to fill in this well of unhappiness.

The analysis could have ended there if we were merely concerned with "shedding light" on the matter. It would have been enough to educate the population and teach the cadres to work more democratically. Some additional investigation led to the question, however: who started the rumor that the death was caused by the well? Was it a mere accident that former landowners dispossessed by the land reform program had spread this rumor? Is it not important to educate the poor peasants to the fact that it was actually their former exploiters who were nurturing their superstitions? Any rectification campaign necessarily results in the unmasking of a certain number of reactionary (or rightist) elements.

Here is another example. The state was having trouble supplying the cities because it purchased rice from the peasants at a price lower than the one offered by the local rice traders. What solution could be found? An increase in prices? In that case, the state would have to sell to the peasants at a higher cost, and prices would never stop spiraling. A campaign of criticism/self-criticism had to be mounted.

In some regions, the price had to be adapted to local conditions. The problem was not just a matter of calculating prices, however. People had to understand that everyone stood to lose if the price of rice were allowed to rise. This was not all. Some people had to set an example by selling their rice at the price set by the state. Farmers who were members of the Workers' Party had to carry out their orders; others would gradually follow their lead. Even then the campaign was not over since the rectification program revealed that there were some people who had aggravated the situation by speculating and deliberately sowing doubt in people's minds. It also uncovered leaders who had given in to pressure from the speculators. Punishing speculators and penalizing negligent cadres is as necessary as adjusting prices, educating peasants, and criticizing the responsible organizations.

Frequently this battle is waged on several fronts. The most important rectification campaign in North Vietnam was waged to correct the errors resulting from the land reform program of 1956-57. During the reform, some peasants were falsely accused or saw their farms plundered, as a result of a particularly radical program put through under especially difficult conditions.

After the completion of the reform, the government and Workers' Party ordered the files reopened, which led to general havoc in each community. Peasants who had recently acquired a recent amount of political awareness were frightened, and returned their plots of land to their former landlords. The latter in turn started all sorts of rumors, encouraging people to believe that the government was about to be overthrown and the old regime restored. The rectification committees were overwhelmed with demands from all sides. The peasants very soon lost their vague notions of their rights, notions painfully acquired during the land reform program, and sank back into their former attitude of resignation.

At the same time, the cities were experiencing extreme shortages. Small businessmen, profiting from the fact that many cadres were being sent to the countryside to correct errors made during land reform, started a wave of wild speculation. Prices soared. Then came the events in Hungary. A group of intellectuals who believed that the era of national and world revolution had ended waged a major campaign to demand art for art's sake and a cultural life free of revolutionary considerations.

Individual cases had to be studied carefully, errors rectified, and the evolution of events explained to everyone; the guilty had to be dealt with harshly, and political guidelines had to be studied more thoroughly. Without the presence everywhere of hundreds of thousands of political activists, without a *mass party* strongly devoted to its principles and aware of the importance of the class struggle, the revolutionary movement would have disintegrated. The mandarins and notables would have come back to power and the country's progress halted for decades. Once this rectification program was completed, matters became greatly clarified in people's minds. Peasants overcame their fear and confusion, and committed themselves wholeheartedly to the cooperative effort.

Social liberation is difficult to accomplish when people can only act in an individual capacity. For example, the law now forbids marriage of girls under 18 years of age. Formerly, however, the custom of marrying them at an early age was widespread. What can a young 15-year-old do when her parents constantly use threats and pleas to force her to marry a man of their choosing—especially when the girl has been raised with the idea that obedience is a child's first duty? The father storms and thunders day in and day out, while her mother bursts into tears every time the subject of marriage is brought up. Night after night the little 15-year-old is accused of being an "ungrateful daughter," the worst possible dishonor in Vietnam.

This matter will not be settled by chairmen of administrative committees or by the courts. The girl now belongs to a youth association which supports her resistance. When she is discouraged, she can seek out her friends. One day the parents will be confronted not only by their daughter but by a delegation of resolute and well-informed young women, and forced to give up their plans.

In a "liberal," individual-oriented regime decades would have passed before principles and laws became reflected in social behavior. A liberal regime is not necessarily a liberating one.

Underdeveloped countries that have been stagnating for centuries are now demanding rapid and profound change in every field. A total restructuring of the foundations and the need for a progressive ideology to overthrow traditional ways of thinking are major priorities. The masses must actively participate in this process and there must be a leading party to guide these masses, a party prepared to deal with all the responsibilities involved. These are the basic conditions for rapid progress.

For the Vietnamese people, Marxism-Leninism has been

an incomparable weapon in the quest for progress. Would other doctrines be equally liberating for other peoples? I obviously cannot claim to know all the answers, but my knowledge of the Vietnamese experience makes me doubt it. Underdeveloped countries need more than economic development, the establishment of political institutions, or the presence of the U.N. They need to solve problems concerning the role of women, the national language, and minority and ethnic groups. Attitudes toward religion, folklore and traditional culture must be redefined. The question of human relations in these countries has to be placed in a new context, and new values and practices must be cultivated.

I personally had the opportunity to live in a feudal society for a long time, and later in an industrialized capitalist country. Now I am actively participating in the building of the new Vietnam. I have yet to find a doctrine which sheds as much light on the various problems of rapid development as does Marxism-Leninism.

The American War: An Interview with JEUNE AFRIQUE

Q: Now that the cease-fire agreement has been signed, what thoughts do you have, after struggling for some thirty years?

A: I believe that it is a very important event. It means that we have brought about the withdrawal of the American forces which tried to bring us to our knees over the past ten years, using every possible means—especially in 1972, which was a terrible year for us. Nonetheless, they were obliged to withdraw. It is a great victory for us. The United States tried everything, and their last resort was the B-52s. They kept thinking they would be able to finish up the war in a few more weeks and each time the deadline had to be postponed. Now we have entered an entirely new stage. We know, however, that dangers still exist since the United States did not sign the agreement without reservations. The U.S. still has enormous resources for another attempt to regain the advantage. But it has tried every possible strategy. It signed the agreement, but it will still keep trying to revert to the situation in 1954 when the Geneva Accords had been signed and the U.S. intervened in the South, immediately launching a bloody repression and massacres in order to wipe out the national movement. The Saigon government is going to try this again, first against the 300,000 political prisoners who are still being held, then against the people. That will be the maneuver. But the situation is completely different now. In 1954, the revolutionary forces withdrew from the South, whereas now one of the essential clauses of the peace agreement is the confirmation and sanction of the presence of a revolutionary government and revolutionary armed forces in the South. The repressive apparatus created by the Americans in the South will not be able to act as it did in 1954.

Objectively, there is victory on the one hand. On the other hand, there are still more pitfalls. Yet the chances of overcoming these pitfalls are good because of the political movement in the South which will put pressure on the Thieu government, in addition to the international movement. The presence of a revolutionary government and armed forces in the South will have to be reckoned with.

Q: According to the agreement, the U.S. must withdraw within 60 days. But what do you think of the possibility of intervention on the part of the Saigon army?

A: The United States will leave the country. The

This interview with Nguyen Khac Vien took place in Paris and was printed in Jeune Afrique *(Young Africa), No. 631, February 10, 1973, under the title, "Vietnam: Un Combattant Explique."*

enormous military and politice apparatus they created will remain. This is significant. One million two hundred thousand men constitute one of the world's largest armies, equipped with ultra-modern weapons, with American instructors. This apparatus will stay behind and it will continue to be financed and armed entirely by the U.S. This machinery has been systematically developed in conformity with American policy all over the third world, with a class of indigenous officers, wholly devoted to Washington. These officers who are paid, trained, instructed and indoctrinated by the U.S. have political positions. They and their families who are in power form a class which is at the same time political, military, commercial and trading, whose purpose it is to wage war and repression.

Ever since his assumption of power in 1969, Nixon has carried out a scorched earth policy, with saturation bombing in the countryside. The entire rural population has been forced to flee to the urban areas. Millions of peasants can no longer work and have no means of making a living. Those who are able-bodied are forced to join the army or the police force. Women have to become prostitutes. Millions of people are shackled to U.S. aid. This is where we meet the greatest problems. Soldiers who do not want to fight have no other means of surviving because the U.S. has destroyed everything. The Saigon army, bureaucrats, police and their families comprise five or six million people out of a total population of seventeen million. We cannot take care of them.

Q: How will this problem be resolved?

A: When peace comes there will be a thaw. People who did not dare speak out, those who did not dare protest, among the civilian population first, then in the army and even the police force later, will begin to stir. With the presence of the revolutionary government to support them, they will regain courage. There will be a very important political struggle. A third force, as it's called, will develop. All those people in the cities who for one reason or another were unable to join the armed struggle will emerge and have their say. We believe that there will be an important political struggle against the Thieu regime. The stubborn hardcore and pro-American forces in the Thieu regime will attempt to unleash a bloody repression. That is certain. Yet there is still a revolutionary army in their very midst, and that will make them think twice.

Q: If the Saigon forces have the perspective which you describe, don't you think that the division of the two zones might be perpetuated?

A: There is a cease-fire in place. The U.S. wanted two zones so that they would be free to do what they please in the zone which they control. But we said no: a cease-fire in place. The sectors will overlap like a "leopard skin." There are risks, but there is also an opportunity to defend peace. If there are hawks among the leaders who would continue their bloody policy, then there will be an important change of heart among the troops.

Q: Yes, but what will happen to the political prisoners whose liberation is not formally covered by the agreement?

A: That is the most immediately sensitive issue, where we must concentrate our political pressure nationally and internationally in the days and weeks to come. The men in power in Saigon are determined to exterminate them all. But the situation is such that they won't succeed, mainly because among these 300,000 political prisoners, there are also friends, cousins of bureaucrats, officers and policemen. World opinion has been alerted.

Q: You referred to the third force. From what you have said, that definition seems to be more sociological than political.

A: In the Saigon-held areas, U.S. influence has been pervasive, with tremendous means at its disposal. There are many people who for one reason or another have been unable to participate in direct struggle, but who, over the course of time, have been forced to take sides.

Take, for example, the people who are well-off, a high-ranking civil servant who lives off American aid. Well, at a given time, his son is obliged to go to war. In the past, sons of wealthy families, students, bureaucrats, were not affected. With Vietnamization, however, everyone is caught up. This was the first crack in the system.

The second blow: daughters carrying on with Americans. This is a moral blow to the family. These people don't want to go to the *maquis*, or join the Front, but they are against U.S. intervention. Hence, here are people, organizations and groups, obviously heterogeneous, which comprise a real force and which bring together a good part of the population.

A place must be made for them because they are there and they form a real force. That is why the Provisional Revolutionary Government assigns an equal place for them, whereas the Americans ignore them as a force.

Q: Some people claim that the peace agreement just signed could have been signed in exactly the same terms much earlier, say in 1969, when Nixon was first inaugurated. Do you agree?

A: It is certain that on our part, from the moment there was a workable agreement allowing us some advantages, we would end the war. Even if it were a compromise, so long as it allowed us to progress. Our most ambitious objective was to make the U.S. leave and to overthrow the Saigon regime. But on a practical level, at a given time, one must accept this or that according to the balance of forces. On the other hand, Washington kept thinking it could bring us to our knees —that's why Nixon tried all the tactics and new weapons first before withdrawing, and it took four years.

Q: Do you think there could be cooperation between Vietnam and the U.S. in the near future?

A: There is an immense hatred of the Americans who have waged war, but it is not directed against the American people. In future cooperation, the U.S. will send people and money. We will accept them. The American game consists of providing aid to create a kind of subversion, whether political, ideological, or simply through corruption. CIA agents will come, but American friends will also come, and we aren't afraid of the CIA. We will be careful.

Q: Yours is at once a socialist country and a third world country. How do you reconcile belonging to these two categories?

A: When I say that we belong to the socialist camp, I don't mean that we follow Soviet and Chinese policies blindly. We follow a policy defined by Marxist analysis.

Q. Is there any neo-colonialism other than American neo-colonialism?

A: It is the most important one. In certain places, it could be French or German, etc. Some friends of the third world claim that American neo-colonialism is less dangerous than another and that there is Soviet neo-colonialism. We tell them frankly that they are mistaken. We say so as Vietnamese first, not as communists. When there is repression, an attempt to eliminate Communist Parties in certain third world countries, this represents a danger not only to communism, but also to national independence in those countries and in other third world countries. Such a policy suppresses one of the forces working for national independence in the world today.

Q: Can Soviet policy sometimes be in contradiction with the interests of certain third world states?

A: There are aspects of Soviet policy which we do not go along with. But basically, the Soviet Union is first and foremost a socialist country as far as we're concerned.

Q: If one were to classify the countries which have helped Vietnam, which would you put first?

A: Let's say that we've been helped a great deal by the socialist countries, the Soviet Union, China and other countries. Then by the progressive countries in Africa and Asia, and the newly independent countries. Finally by the workers and the democratic movement for peace all over the world, including the U.S.

Q: Do you expect much Soviet assistance in reconstruction?

A: Of course, we have long-term plans with the Soviet Union and other socialist countries, whereas we can't have these plans with capitalist countries.

Q: How long do you think reconstruction will take?

A: It's difficult to say, because we've got to rebuild differently than before and we don't know the extent of foreign aid yet. We estimate that within 15 years we'll be able to attain a decent standard of living.

Q: What is the extent of destruction in the Democratic Republic of Vietnam?

A: In 1972, the U.S. tried to destroy the entire economic infrastructure of the North. All the cities were hit. As far as residential areas are concerned, not one town was left intact. Each town, each factory and each bridge will have to be rebuilt.

Why Nixon Bombed Hanoi

Q: Can you describe the December bombing which you witnessed?

A: From the American side, this offensive was undertaken with the objective of obtaining major concessions on the October version of the peace agreement. We turned them down. It was a matter of principle, no question about it. Do what you please, we told them, we won't give in. So they launched their B-52s on the evening of December 18. Le Duc Tho arrived in Hanoi that afternoon. At eight in the evening, the bombing started. The first week they pounded the periphery, the rail marshalling yards and surrounding villages. The radio station was also attacked at the beginning. They tried to wipe it out so that our voice would no longer be heard around the world.

The B-52s came during the night. During the daytime, they used very accurate fighter-bombers to find missile launching pads and to strike economic targets.

It was quite impressive to see the missiles firing. The whole sky was illuminated. Why do I say impressive? Because of the absence of panic or terror. The Americans were unable to create the panic they would have wished in order to force the DRV government to yield.

Q: Can you estimate the number of victims?

A: In the thousands. The bombing on the 26th, the day after Christmas, was the most deadly. Fifty B-52s came, accompanied by about 40 fighter planes. These bombings had the main purpose of forcing us to capitulate or to make very important concessions. They had the secondary purpose of inflicting as much destruction as possible in order to prevent construction, so that they could say, "That is where socialism leads!"

Q: Why did the U.S. have to renege on the October 26 agreement in such an appalling manner?

A: They were first pressured by the elections. Everything had to be finished before the elections, so that Nixon could appear victorious. Hence the earlier saturation bombings, much heavier than in 1967-68, with the Haiphong blockade, bombings, diplomatic maneuvers to isolate us, and even counterfeit money dropped from planes to throw our economy into disarray. In July and August of 1972, they thought they could finish us off by bombing the dikes. It would have really been dreadful if there had been flooding of the delta accompanied by continuous bombardment. Luckily there had been no rain, and the water level was four meters lower than in 1971.

Surrounding the delta, which has fifteen million inhabitants, there are mountainous regions ten times the size of the delta. When it rains, the water collects in the delta basin and rises very rapidly. For thousands of years, we have built dikes, ten to 14 meters high, about 2,400 miles long in all. The United States started bombing the dikes along the seashore. When sea water penetrates the rice paddies, it takes at least five or six years to get rid of the salt. Then they bombed all the weak links of the river dikes. They bombed the sluices. Often they used really huge bombs targeted alongside the dike. The dike itself would not be hit, but the result would be cracks which were very hard to repair.

So, they thought we would be obliged to capitulate. Since we continued to resist and since their elections were fast approaching, we presented them our version of the agreement. With the elections so near, they were forced to accept it. Once reelected, Nixon reneged, pretending for the sake of the American public that the details had to be revised. They let us know that if we didn't come to terms they would send B-52s. For us, however, it was a basic issue.

Q: Could we try to define the U.S. motives during this war? By definition, isn't this an unproductive war for them?

A: Obviously it's not the economic exploitation of Indochina and Vietnam which can bring them back the 200 billion dollars they have spent. Even if the U.S. exploited Indochina for a thousand years, they couldn't recoup their losses. So there must be another reason for U.S. intervention.

That reason can be traced to a global strategy of counterrevolution promulgated by Washington at the end of World War II. In 1945, the U.S. assumed the "white man's burden." Socialist countries were established, and socialist revolution threatened to spread. National liberation revolutions were growing. Movements for peace and democracy were developing in capitalist countries.

All of this constituted a worldwide revolutionary movement which threatened all capitalist countries, and the U.S. found itself leading the defense of the capitalist world. Its global strategy of counterrevolution was aimed first against the Soviet Union which in 1945, greatly weakened by the war, did not have the atomic bomb and was isolated. The U.S. was immeasurably stronger.

From 1945 to 1950, the U.S. was not interested in third world countries such as India, but in Iran and Turkey, countries having a common border with the Soviet Union, and which could serve as military bases. This strategy became obsolete after the fall of Chiang Kai-shek. Socialist countries in Eastern Europe gained stability, and the Soviet Union developed the atomic bomb. A direct attack against these great socialist countries would have been dangerous for the U.S. So Washington turned its global strategy against the third world countries.

The gradual reversal took a decisive turn with Kennedy. Reread *Strategy of Peace*. The techniques, weapons and tactics to crush national liberation movements are outlined there. Once third world countries were conquered and under U.S. tutelage, then the socialist camp would be isolated. Hence, Vietnam was a stumbling block. There the war of national liberation took its classic form. It had to be crushed to serve as an example and to test all the various weapons, tactics and forms of military activity. It was necessary to suppress Vietnam so that fear of the U.S. could be maintained all over the world.

They proceeded in stages. At each stage they advanced certain methods, thinking that they would be enough. From 1950 to 1954 they helped the French with arms and dollars in an attempt to wipe us out. That didn't work. Second stage: 1954-1960. First the total liquidation of the national and revolutionary movement in the South. Our troops were evacuated and the population was terrorized. They thought they could firmly install a puppet regime in the South and then relaunch the war of conquest against the North. This was a terrible time. The people of the South were struggling for peace and the militants were being massacred from 1954 to 1959. We were bound by the Geneva Accords. We didn't want to issue the order for armed struggle. With our bare hands we had to fight those who were slaughtering us. It was a much harder time than the later bombings.

Subsequently, people went on to armed struggle. The Diem regime collapsed. The U.S. passed into another phase in 1961. They attempted what they called special warfare: massively equipping and reinforcing the Saigon army, raising it to 500,000 men with electronic equipment, helicopters, artillery, tanks and 25,000 American advisers. First they tried to eliminate the regular troop units of the National Liberation Front, and then they relocated the population. Against these armed units, the chosen weapon was the helicopter. They felt it was the ultimate weapon in combating guerrillas. They herded people into strategic hamlets—"draining the water," they said, "to catch the fish."

That was the policy, but it was a fiasco by 1965. People took steps to protect themselves. So the United States had to resort to other methods. On August 5, 1964, the first warning was sent to North Vietnam: the first bombing. If you do not cease your activities, they said, the bombings will continue. In February 1965, saturation bombing of the North began, and U.S. troops landed in South Vietnam. During the first year, 1965, there were 180,000 soldiers. They thought this would suffice.

A Collapsing Policy

Q: They said at that time that it was a matter of saving the South Vietnamese government which was on the verge of collapse.

A: They had to save an entire policy which was collapsing. Massive bombing raids against the North, Marines landing in the South. All of this to make us accept their conditions quickly. In vain. In October 1965, there were some 700,000 men in the Saigon army, and 180,000 Americans in South Vietnam, plus the Seventh Fleet offshore. The U.S.-Saigon forces launched a counteroffensive during the dry season of 1965-66 to destroy the pockets of resistance and annihilate the main regular units. This lasted from October until April without any success. So they had to bring in reinforcements in 1966. At the end of 1966 U.S. troops numbered 400,000 men. They even launched a second offensive to attempt the same objective.

Once again, it failed. In 1967, they brought still more reinforcements, and their numbers rose to 540,000. However, despite these reinforcements, this time no major counter-offensive was launched as in 1965-66. That was significant.

In 1968 we launched the Tet offensive. It was

not so much to retake the cities as to show that the presence of 540,000 Americans was meaningless. We could be everywhere in spite of 540,000 Americans. Also counting Saigon, Korean, Thai and other troops, the total was 1,300,000 men. Despite all that, we were on the offensive in every city. *The Wall Street Journal* concluded at that point that the U.S. could not win. Johnson accepted the Paris Conference, while preparing yet another policy which Nixon would carry out: Vietnamization. To Vietnamize is to destroy the countryside and force everyone to join the army. The U.S. expeditionary forces could have withdrawn within a few months. But they had to wait four years, supporting and reinforcing the Saigon forces which consist of 1,200,000 men including the police.

Sihanouk's "sanctuary" remained, however. His neutralist government was a source of irritation because it interrupted the Bangkok-Phnom Penh-Saigon axis. The U.S. thought that its *coup d'etat* against Sihanouk and the Cambodian invasion would deal a fatal blow to the Vietnamese resistance, and at the same time bring the Cambodians over to their side, thus killing two birds with one stone. A mistake! It didn't occur to them that there had been continuous resistance to French colonialism in Cambodia, that there was also a revolutionary party, and that Cambodia had been implementing an independent policy against the U.S. for 15 years. The *coup d'etat* aroused Cambodian national feeling, and resistance was far more vigorous than they ever expected. Sihanouk was first of all a patriot, then a prince. They lost out. They plan failed; another front had opened up.

South Vietnamese resistance could henceforth count on the Cambodian resistance. By 1971, there was thus a Lao-Cambodian-South Vietnamese resistance, along with North Vietnam, a total of four fronts against U.S. colonization. The communications lifeline of these fronts, however, went through southern Laos. Saigon forces, with their American allies, wanted to destroy this line of communications. This was the occasion to test the best Saigon divisions, particularly those formed from 1969 onward.

So in early 1971 they launched an operation on Route 8, with American divisions protecting the rear, concentrating 2,000 planes and helicopters over an area of 30 miles.

Route 8 runs between two hill ranges. They occupied the hills using helicopters. We had foreseen the strike. We waited for them. When the helicopters landed, they were greeted by our artillery fire. What a slaughter! Several hundred helicopters and everything they had parachuted onto the hills.

Yet they kept a solid belt of fortifications, and a tough pacification effort was being carried out in the countryside. Then we launched the offensive of March 1972. Our artillery and tanks took them by surprise. They claimed to control the entire jungle, not allowing a single fly to get through. Our tanks got through.

We were able to penetrate this defense line first and then block all the best divisions of the Saigon army. Guerrillas were able to regain ground little by little on the plains. The 1972 offensive was not so much an offensive to conquer land as to neutralize the Saigon army and allow the reinvigoration of guerrilla warfare.

Furthermore, it should not be said that Nixon's bombing of the North was simply a response to this offensive. Even if there had been no offensive, the bombings would have taken place. Because they wanted an end to the war. Fighting continues in the South, which means that there are still pretexts for bombing the North. Here is how events took place progressively from one phase to the next. From 1950 to 1954, U.S. collusion with the crumbling colonial power; from 1954 to 1959, bloody repression and massacres to try to eliminate the revolutionary movement. From 1960 to 1965, special warfare. From 1965 to 1969, war waged by U.S. troops. From 1969 to 1972, "Vietnamization." In 1972, the final means of all. After B-52s, there doesn't seem to be anything more they can do. Apparently they have come to their technological limit.

Three Currents of Revolution

Q: According to this interpretation, everything comes out very neatly, but isn't there also a Vietnamese strategy?

A: Let me tell you about 1965, which was a crucial year for us. While the U.S. was bombing the North, it was landing troops in the South. At that time, many of our friends around the world despaired. But we told ourselves: on a global scale, worldwide revolution is on the offensive, and it's American imperialism which is on the defensive. American imperialism had to confront a three-pronged revolutionary movement. We call it the three currents of revolution—socialist countries, national liberation movements, and the workers' movements for peace and democracy inside capitalist countries. The convergence of these three currents means that our struggle occurred at a time when imperialism had to fight defensively. We are no longer in the nineteenth century. Of course, there are still *coup d'etats* now and then. Regimes fall and align themselves with imperialism, but on the whole, imperialism is on the defensive.

Within this framework, a national liberation movement has the opportunity and the means, even if it initially seems feeble and poorly armed, to take hold and to advance. In the case of Vietnam, when French troops landed in Saigon in 1945, although they were not as powerful as the U.S. in 1965, we were obliged to adopt temporarily a defensive strategy, ceding the cities, Hanoi and Saigon, and retreating to the countryside and jungles.

It was a very demanding strategy. Imagine this recently formed liberation movement with ardent youths who gave up their rice in order to buy guns and who saw French troops burning their villages and raping their women. It was very hard on them—but the strategy had to be carried out.

Would we do the same thing in 1965? No. The situation had changed. We were on the offensive.

The U.S. landed in a position of weakness, to meet a foregone defeat. Saigon's army had almost been beaten. Thus we did not have to retreat. We used an offensive strategy in attacking the Americans from the moment they landed, right where they got off. That was the strategic command. Do not give up any territory or withdraw. Stay right on top of the Americans. The guerrillas must stand by the people, the people must stay with the land— no one is to give in.

The U.S. military apparatus is very powerful, very strong, but it also has fissures, weaknesses and deficiencies. Instead of being impressed, look for the weaknesses. Those who panic and close their eyes won't be able to see.

Some have said, "The U.S. is bombing, we should help the South, defend the North. All our efforts must be concentrated on the war. Stop building socialism. It's folly to do both things at the same time. We aren't strong enough." We disagreed. We must do both things at the same time— mobilize the people for the resistance, for the counterattack, while continuing to build socialism. The enemy can't use all his strength. Technologically he could have, but politically he couldn't. Therefore, we had the time and means to prepare to strike.

Socialism is now part of the national consciousness. Patriotism can only develop when the country is oriented toward socialism, the yeast of national feeling. If that is stunted, then national feeling itself will lose half its vigor. For example, if serious ecological research were abandoned while the U.S. continued bombing, the army would gain a few young recruits but you would have suppressed a motivation for patriotism.

Thus, the directive to the universities was not to stop enrollment but, on the contrary, to increase it. The number of students at the universities rose from 26,000 in 1965 to 70,000 in 1970. We have sent far more students abroad to socialist countries during this period than ever before. When we requested cannons and microscopes from our friends, some told us: "We can give you all the cannons you want, but microscopes . . . be reasonable!"

We maintained this directive at the universities: increase

enrollment. But we said: don't stay in Hanoi, go to the villages and mountains. How? Figure out a way. Through this strategic directive, therefore, we were able to mobilize all the energy and initiative of the intelligentsia.

Q: How does one go about "figuring out a way"?

A: We have a general political and strategic orientation which must be strictly followed. We can see this most concretely at the grass roots level. Party organizations in the villages are in charge of seeing that the village administrative committees implement the political line, not that they carry out certain instructions from the ministries. In the South, it is a threefold struggle: political, military, and a persuasion campaign amidst the enemy. For instance, a young female worker lays a mine on the road. After that she continues to work. A jeep lands on the mine. A Saigon soldier is wounded. She runs up to look after him and while talking to him, asks questions like, "Why are you fighting for the Americans?" That evening she talks to her cousin who is an officer. Another time she participates in a demonstration.

American artillery shells a village. People flee, dispersing via trenches through the fields. When the shelling stops, the Americans think that there is no more resistance, and an American or Saigon patrol enters the village. People have come back through the tunnel by now, however, and only a dozen men are needed to decimate a battalion.

Q: Don't you think that by 1972 Vietnamization had partially, if not completely, succeeded?

A: U.S. participation continued in other forms. There had been neither a military nor a general disengagement. U.S. ground forces were no longer involved, but the Air Force and Navy participated more heavily with more lethal weapons. The bombings were far more barbaric in 1972. In a certain sense they succeeded. When they try a new tactic, a new weapon, they are always successful at the beginning. It takes time for us to find an antidote.

Q: You are part of the socialist camp. Therefore, you have an alliance, even if it's not formal on a military level, especially with the larger socialist states. Don't you feel that these countries, particularly the Soviet Union, were wrong when they accepted the aggression of 1965 as not being serious enough to warrant vigorous reaction?

A: For the Soviet Union, blocking aggression against Vietnam has a military side and a political side. In our country, on our national territory, all the great contradictions of our age converge: first, the contradiction between imperialism and socialism; second, the contradiction between imperialism and national liberation; and third, the contradiction between the various classes within our country.

The most important of these for us is the second.

We have refused volunteers from Russia and China. Pilots would have been very useful to us, for instance, but we turned them down. Why? If we had allowed the confrontation of Soviet and American pilots, it would have been a confrontation of socialism and capitalism. Now, we do not want to change the imperialist-nationalist contradiction into an imperialist-socialist contradiction. What is secondary should not be changed into the primary consideration. That is why we asked for technical and material assistance, but not for men. We did not ask the Soviet Union to start a war elsewhere. One cannot say, ourselves first, and to hell with everyone else. There are thousands of ways to help Vietnam. American imperialism is somewhat like Gulliver; it must be tied with all sorts of strings, and not just with warfare.

The Old Banyan Tree

I found out one day in February 1962 that the old banyan tree in our village had just been chopped down, sacrificed to the widening of the road leading into the village. The disappearance of the old banyan tree from the landscape. has taken a big chunk out of my childhood, yet the widening of the road fulfills a dream I have nurtured for some thirty years.

When I was a child, we used to go almost every day and sit at the foot of the banyan as the sun went down, to enjoy the cool evening breeze after the heat of the summer day. Actually, the banyan was more of an edifice than a tree. It took eight or ten of us children hooked together to reach around its enormous trunk, gnarled and hollowed out. Its branches were even bigger than the pillars of the village pagoda, and they rose so high in the sky that we could barely see the big birds perched on top. The roots came up from the ground like angry snakes, twisted, knotted, furrowed with deep wrinkles.

The wind blowing in from the fields played a strange music through the branches, and we thought we could hear above us sighings and simperings, laughter and moans. We could look out and see the ripening rice waving in the evening breeze. The croaking of the frogs heralded the coming of the night, while the buffalo, with half-naked children perched on their backs, returned home along meandering paths with a heavy, slow and swinging gait. The shadows of their horns lengthened over the drowsy fields.

As the seasons changed, the rice fields took on different colors and smells. We used to slip in between the fragrant rice stalks during the summer harvest and catch golden-jaw grasshoppers, which we would string on a rice stem underneath the cuirasses of their necks, bringing home skewers full of them. When the fields were dry and cracked, and could produce no crops, we used to race across followed by barking dogs, pursuing homemade kites borne off by the wind. After the rice seedlings had been transplanted we used to sit at the foot of the banyan tree, gazing entranced at the glimmering fields, the rows of young plants quivering under the caress of the wind and stretching as far as the horizon. When the nearby river overflowed, the plain turned into an immense lake, and we would row happily over to neighboring villages to visit our relatives.

At harvest time, the rice was spread out on the large brick drying-yard next to our house. Men harnessed themselves to a heavy stone roller and pulled it all day long in this

This essay was originally published in Vietnam Courier, *August 31, 1970.*

yard which became overheated by the summer sun. Sweat
trickled down their naked backs. But we were absorbed by
an indefinable intoxication with the smell of the new rice,
the dust, the summer heat, and the continuous drone of the
stone roller crushing the rice stems.

With the rice brought in, it was time to drain the family
pond. Men began to work the scoops at dawn, pouring water
out into adjoining fields. Toward late afternoon, the muddy
bottom of the pond could at last be seen, teeming with fish,
and we jumped down and plopped into the water, squealing
with joy. With mud up to our navels, we caught the fish by
the handful and threw them into baskets which the women
carried to the house. The pond was completely drained by
nightfall, and when we returned to the yard the women went
to one corner to divide up the fish. Now, nearly thirty years
later, I can still remember the smell of carp and catfish, and
hear the whispers of the women discussing the distribution of
the fish parts.

How I loved my village! It was not like a town where
everyone lives by himself. Here, everyone knew everyone
else. The children played together in groups of several dozen.
People got together each festival day at the temples of their
ancestors. I could go visit an uncle or an aunt several miles
away for several days without my parents worrying in the
least. If a house was being built, everybody was there, and we
children would romp about, try the saw for cutting up
planks, mix the mortar, and roll in the sawdust and wood
shavings. In the evening when the moonlight was bright, we
used to gather at the crossroads and watch wrestling matches.
Big burly fellows, clad in loincloths, grappled with each other
and tried to fling their opponents to the ground, to everyone's cheers. One festival followed another: anniversaries for
the ancestors, processions in honor of the village guardian
spirit, ceremonies to appease wandering souls, weddings,
funerals. Every occasion was an opportunity for getting
together, gossiping, discussing, gambling and eating.

In winter we would sit up late at night peeling and

cutting areca nuts. Grouped around big bamboo trays under a kerosene lamp hanging from the ceiling, we talked to each other in a lively manner. As the conversation died down further into the night and everyone started to feel sleepy, someone would shout, "Ong Chau, please recite us a story!" His goatee quivering with pleasure, Ong Chau would wait for us to insist a bit more, and then he would clear his throat. A hush fell, and in the still of the night, the old man in his melodic voice would start to tell us the misfortunes of the enchanting Kieu. Her beauty made the flowers envious and her talents outshone those of all the artists and poets of her time, yet her fate was one of the worst, her tribulations the most severe, on account of that very beauty. We listened to Ong Chau recite her story with adulation, for, although he was illiterate, he knew the story of Kieu by heart, all 3,524 lines of it.[1]

How I loved my village! Yet only a few weeks' stay would fill me with a feeling of depression. I was the only one who owned a bicycle, a shiny one with nickel-plated parts, but what a strain it was to go over the tortuous paths full of potholes and bumps, strewn with thorns. There had never been a need before for straight and wide roads. People were used to going everywhere on foot. Everything was carried on men's—or, more often, women's—backs, including rice, manure, sand and bricks. After it rained you had to grip the clay paths with your toes to avoid slipping and falling. The sides of the paths were strewn with excrement, which the rain carried into the pond from where the drinking water was drawn. Rubbish accumulated in the market place in huge piles around which swarmed big green flies.

I was terribly embarrassed when I passed by old men in the village and they took off their hats when they saw me coming, bowing their heads, and greeting me with a respect-

---

[1] *The Tale of Kieu*, written in the early nineteenth century, is easily the most famous and best-loved work in Vietnamese literature.— *Ed.*

ful "Honorable mandarin's son." I was deeply angered by the money people spent on processions to plead for rain from the rain god, or to try to appease the cholera god, and by the practice of "curing" illnesses with joss-stick ashes or holy water from the temples. When my father ordered me to put on a turban to go to the village hall and attend ceremonies in honor of the guardian spirits, it was real torture. After an endless ritual, the village notables sat down to a banquet, got drunk, hurled abuse at each other, and tried to pull out each other's hair. (Some men still wore their hair in a bun.) Each notable competed with the others to bring home the head of the sacrificial chicken from the ceremony because in the eyes of his wife, children and neighbors this would be irrefutable proof that he was the most honored man in the village. None of these notables read a newspaper, and there had never been any films shown in the vilallage. No one knew anything about electricity, sports or machines. And how many times had I seen young 15-year-old girls, my cousins, weeping from the bottoms of their hearts because they were forced to marry men they had never even seen before!

People knew only one thing about the outside world— that they had to pay taxes to the French, who were reputed to have yellow hair and pointed noses. It was rumored at low voices that disobedient villages had been razed to the ground by these same French people and that their power was overwhelming.

How often, sitting at the foot of the banyan tree and listening to the eerie music of the wind in its branches, had I dreamed of widening the roads, cleaning up the ponds, combating the superstitions, suppressing those drunken and quarrelsome notables, and abolishing child marriages.

But in those days, all I could do was dream. Of course I knew my village like the back of my hand. I knew every hollow on the edge of the pond, where you could catch fish as they slipped in to sleep at dusk. I could recognize every dog in the village by its bark, and I knew everything that happened in the families of my young friends.

But still I had to wait until the land reform was carried out and the land was redistributed to the peasants before I really knew my village. Now that the curtain was down, I could see what was actually going on backstage. Those rice fields which changed with the seasons were our rice fields and belonged to my family and my clan. As landowners, they were masters of the village. I used to naively believe that the honor shown to my family came from the scholarly achievements of my father, a worthy disciple of the Great Master, Confucius. I did not know that the men who did the harvesting while I hunted my grasshoppers, the men who pulled the stone rollers over our drying-yard under a searing sun, the men who floundered in the bottom of the fish pond, were all tenants hired by my family. I did not know that after an exhausting day scooping water out of a well-stocked pond, they were only allowed to take home some small fry to their wives and children, while our kitchen table overflowed with succulent carp and catfish. I did not know that when Ong Chau came to our house to peel areca nuts and recite verses about the misfortunes of Kieu, he was not paid, because as a tenant farmer it was one of his obligations to tell us stories. I did not know that when we happily sailed over the flooded fields or raced behind our kites on the drought-cracked soil, the hearts of the village people were full of anguish because they would have to come to our house to borrow rice and money which they would be obliged to repay at the next harvest at twice the amount.

There came a time when I stopped dreaming. The tortuous, excrement-strewn paths, the superstitions, the disputes between notables, the child marriages have all disappeared now, or are about to disappear, because land rents and usurious interest rates have vanished and the rice fields have been disributed to those who formerly had none. My family lost all its rice fields, but the dreams I had in my childhood have come true, one by one, before my very eyes.

The roads have been widened and there are wheelbarrows and carts on them now. The number of bicycles has multiplied. Not everyone has his own newspaper, but the village cooperative has a book collection and subscribes to reviews and journals. The wind no longer plays its weird music in the branches of the old banyan, but on moonlit nights you can hear young people singing. Heated discussions on who will get the head of the chicken no longer occur, but discussions do take place on how to transplant rice, make plows, dig irrigation canals or set up a day care center. And today just try to force a young girl to marry a man she does not love!

I don't have any regrets about the banyan tree of my childhood. Each year, when *Tet*[2] comes and the peasants take time off from their work in the fields, President Ho Chi Minh goes out to plant some trees, with young and old alike following his example throughout the country. Our villages will be much greener than they were before.

In the old days, I would have refused the request of a foreign friend if he had asked me to take him on a visit to my village, fearing he would see the piles of rubbish the market place, the drunken notables and the child marriages. But now, I heartily welcome all men from the "four oceans" to visit my village, our villages.

[2] The Lunar New Year festival, celebrated sometime between January and March, depending on the lunar cycle.—*Ed.*

Other Publications Available from the Indochina Resource Center

Vietnam: What Kind of Peace? Full-text and careful analysis of the 1973 Paris Agreement on Vietnam. $1.50.

Indochina Chronicle. Monthly newsletter of the Indochina Resource Center. Each issue deals with a separate topic. $5.00 per year. Back issues also available.

Indochina Today. Comprehensive monthly compendium of news articles from English, French and Vietnamese-language sources. Together with a four-page summary, *The U.S. in Indochina,* this is available for $25.00 per year.

Hostages of War: Saigon's Political Prisoners. by Holmes Brown and Don Luce. $1.50

Children's Series:

Banh Chung Banh Day (The New Year's Rice Cakes). An ancient Vietnamese tale depicting the shift from hunting to agricultural pursuits. 50 cents.

Children of Vietnam. by Tran Khanh Tuyet. Vignettes and drawings of daily life. 75 cents.

The Tale of Tam and Cam. A popular Vietnamese folktale akin to Cinderella. Available after July, 1974.

Phu Dong Thien Vuong (The Child Hero of Dong Village). A bronze-age folktale of resistance to alien invasion. Available after November, 1974.

Order from:

Indochina Resource Center
P.O. Box 4000-D
Berkeley, Ca. 94704